GCSE
MATHS
PRACTICE 1

Rosalind Hollis

Cassell Publishers Limited
Artillery House
Artillery Row
London SW1P 1RT

First published 1989

British Library Cataloguing in Publication Data

Hollis, R. G. (Rosalind G.)
  GCSE maths practice 1.
  1. Mathematics
  I. Title
  510

  ISBN 0-304-31746-2
        0-304-31749-7 (with answers)

Typeset in Futura and Times Roman by Fakenham Photosetting Limited,
Fakenham, Norfolk
Printed and bound in Great Britain by Billing & Sons Ltd., Worcester

Designed by Vaughan Allen

contents

preface

This series is written for the prospective lower and middle GCSE ability range (grades D to G). All the topics required for these levels by the various examination boards are included.

The items from List 1 of the National Criteria (1985) are covered thoroughly both with mechanical practice and applications in simple problem solving.

All the items from List 2 are covered using simple examples and applications appropriate to pupils who may be entered at the intermediate level.

The basic processes are covered thoroughly in graded exercises which allow pupils to gain confidence and demonstrate positive achievement. The worked examples at the top of the pages will serve as a reminder. They do not presuppose any teaching method.

All the work on each part of the syllabus is grouped together. Teachers will wish to make selections appropriate to their pupils' needs. Each page is self contained to allow as much flexibility as possible.

Some exercises are written to encourage the use of approximations and to develop a feel for number, length, weight, etc. Intelligent use of a calculator is encouraged.

Practical and everyday situations are widely used. Familiarity with both metric units and the imperial measures in common use is assumed. Clear and direct questions are used to encourage pupils to start exploring each problem. Some of the situations lend themselves to class discussion. Others may easily be developed into investigations.

The papers of mixed practice have been constructed so that there are parallel papers. Thus, if children have done a paper, and then worked on the parts they found difficult, they can then do the next paper with confidence that their score will be much improved because it covers exactly the same material.

The author and publishers wish to thank the pupils and the staff of the Mathematics Department of Sarah Metcalfe School, Cleveland, for their help in the preparation of this book.

R. G. Hollis, October 1988

1 number

The multiples of 3 are 3, 6, 9, 12, . . .

The square of 5 is 25.

2, 3, 5, 7, 11, 13, 17, . . . are prime numbers.

The cube of 5 is $5 \times 5 \times 5 = 125$.

A Write down the multiples of:

1 3, which are less than 20
2 5, which are less than 21
3 2, which are less than 13
4 4, which are less than 25
5 6, which are less than 20
6 7, which are less than 50
7 8, which are less than 45
8 9, which are less than 70
9 6, which are between 40 and 65
10 8, which are between 50 and 84

Which of these are multiples of:

11 3: 6, 14, 15, 18?
12 5: 5, 10, 12?
13 4: 4, 6, 8, 12?
14 3: 3, 7, 9, 18, 21?
15 4: 16, 22, 24?
16 7: 14, 24, 28, 35?
17 6: 18, 30, 35?
18 8: 24, 40, 56, 60?
19 9: 45, 49, 63, 81?
20 5: 75, 45, 54, 80?

B Write down the odd multiples of:

1 7, which are between 20 and 70
2 9, which are between 30 and 60
3 5, which are between 73 and 94
4 8, which are between 60 and 86
5 6, which are between 20 and 50

Write down the even multiples

6 9, which are less than 60
7 7, which are less than 50
8 11, which are less than 84
9 5, which are between 24 and 64
10 7, which are between 30 and 60

Which of these are prime numbers?

11 13, 17, 27
12 31, 23, 49
13 7, 91, 47
14 17, 31, 81
15 13, 67, 97

Write down the prime numbers:

16 between 4 and 10
17 between 10 and 20
18 between 20 and 40
19 between 40 and 70
20 between 70 and 100

C Write down the square of:

1 4
2 5
3 3
4 6
5 2

6 7
7 1
8 9
9 8
10 10

D Write down the cube of:

1 4
2 3
3 2
4 6
5 8

6 7
7 0
8 9
9 1
10 10

E Write in figures:

1 two thousand and one
2 five thousand and twelve
3 eight hundred and twenty
4 fifteen thousand and thirty
5 twelve thousand and sixty

6 nine hundred and five
7 fifty thousand three hundred and two
8 eighty thousand and fifty-three
9 six hundred point five
10 seventy point nought four

A Write as products:

1	10	**11**	55
2	8	**12**	20
3	9	**13**	49
4	12	**14**	25
5	15	**15**	54
6	21	**16**	24
7	6	**17**	44
8	25	**18**	30
9	18	**19**	77
10	24	**20**	48

B Write as products of prime factors:

1	8	**11**	30
2	18	**12**	84
3	21	**13**	60
4	42	**14**	192
5	24	**15**	63
6	36	**16**	88
7	28	**17**	128
8	70	**18**	176
9	81	**19**	162
10	48	**20**	144

C Write down the square root of:

1	16	**6**	25
2	36	**7**	100
3	9	**8**	49
4	81	**9**	64
5	1	**10**	144

D What is the 9 worth?

1	95	**6**	296
2	943	**7**	789
3	596	**8**	47.9
4	1792	**9**	58.91
5	9314	**10**	3.94

E

1 What is the greatest prime factor of 39?
2 What is the largest even factor of 84?
3 What is the product of two odd numbers?
4 Write down the square root of 81.
5 What is the square of 12?
6 What is the product of an odd and an even number?
7 What is the greatest prime factor of 66?
8 How many primes are there between 10 and 20?
9 Write down the square of 8.
10 Write down the square root of 49.

11 Write down an odd factor of 24.
12 Write down an even factor of 14.
13 Write down a prime factor of 20.
14 Write down a prime factor of 44.
15 Write down an odd factor of 28.
16 Write down a prime factor of 63.
17 When an odd number is multiplied by an even number what will be the answer?
18 $A \times 6 = 143$. A is a whole number. How do you know 143 is the wrong answer?
19 Write down a prime factor of 42.
20 Write down an odd factor of 56.

EXAMPLE

$3^2 = 9$

$2^3 = 8$

$\sqrt{9} = 3$

In the number 273.7 the 7s mean 7 tens and 7 tenths. The first 7 is worth 100 times the second 7.

A Find the value of:

1 4^2
2 3^3
3 5^2
4 2^3
5 5^3
6 1^2
7 10^2
8 30^2
9 8^2
10 6^2

11 3^2
12 1^3
13 $\sqrt{16}$
14 2^2
15 $\sqrt{4}$
16 0^2
17 20^2
18 10^3
19 $\sqrt{100}$
20 6^3

B Write down the value of the 3 in each of these:

1 30
2 135
3 7300
4 5030
5 6.3
6 5.63
7 4.03
8 16.3
9 135 000
10 2.003

C Use the signs $<, \leqslant, >, \geqslant, =, \neq$ to make true statements.

1 2×5 11
2 3×5 11
3 7×2.9 21
4 4.7×8 40
5 5.1×9.1 45

6 3^2 10
7 3.1^2 10
8 3.2^2 10
9 4.4^2 20
10 4.5^2 20

11 6^2 40
12 6.1^2 40
13 6.2^2 40
14 2^3 8
15 $\sqrt{16}$ 8

D

| | | | | | | | | | | |
|0|1|2|3|4|5|6|7|8|9|

Write down the whole numbers for which x could make these inequalities true:

1 $0 < x < 4$
2 $2 < x \leqslant 6$
3 $1 < x < 7$
4 $3 \leqslant x < 5$
5 $6 < x < 9$

6 $1 < x \leqslant 3$
7 $5 < x < 8$
8 $0 < x \leqslant 3$
9 $0 < 2x < 5$
10 $3 < 2x \leqslant 8$

11 $4 < 2x < 8$
12 $6 < 2x < 9$
13 $0 < 2x < 8$
14 $0 < 3x < 7$
15 $1 < 3x \leqslant 9$

E Write the next two numbers in each sequence:

1 $3x$: 15, 18, 21, ...
2 x^2: 25, 36, 49, ...
3 $2x^2$: 2, 8, 18, ...
4 x^3: 1, 8, 27, ...
5 $3x^2$: 3, 12, 27, ...

EXAMPLE
$23 \times 200 = 2300 \times 2 = 4600$ $826 \div 200 = 8.26 \div 2 = 4.13$

A
1. 23×100
2. 57×100
3. 465×10
4. 892×100
5. 37×100
6. 24×20
7. 31×300
8. 53×40
9. 64×200
10. 432×30
11. 572×300
12. 689×90
13. 525×40
14. 625×300
15. 765×80
16. 85×60
17. 76×500
18. 347×400
19. 320×70
20. 158×50

B
1. $408 \div 20$
2. $680 \div 10$
3. $7600 \div 20$
4. $850 \div 100$
5. $7820 \div 100$
6. $5648 \div 100$
7. $486 \div 30$
8. $684 \div 40$
9. $792 \div 300$
10. $6180 \div 600$
11. $5616 \div 80$
12. $4907 \div 70$
13. $496 \div 80$
14. $8910 \div 900$
15. $5810 \div 70$
16. $4680 \div 900$
17. $728 \div 80$
18. $6848 \div 400$
19. $6300 \div 50$
20. $89\,460 \div 90$

C
1. $640 \div 20$
2. 450×40
3. 64×500
4. 460×60
5. $3780 \div 900$
6. 250×400
7. $6450 \div 500$
8. 4870×200
9. $783 \div 90$
10. $5800 \div 2000$
11. $360 \div 30$
12. 25×70
13. $4800 \div 40$
14. 87×300
15. 35×80
16. $11\,070 \div 90$
17. $19\,600 \div 700$
18. 62×800
19. $31\,500 \div 60$
20. $260\,000 \div 400$

D

1. What is the next whole number after 5099?

2. What is the remainder when 1640 is divided by 7?

3. Write down the next two numbers in the sequence 5, 25, 125, . . .

4. From the numbers 5, 15, 25, 35, 45, 55, write down: (a) a multiple of 3,
   (b) a square number,
   (c) a prime number,
   (d) the next number in the sequence 5, 15, 25, 35, . . .

5. Two girls have to pack eggs in boxes of six. How many boxes will they need for 480 eggs?

6. The chairs in a hall are arranged so there are 7 on one side of the aisle and 8 on the other side in the front row. All the rows behind are the same. How many rows are needed for 240 chairs?

7. Two bags each contain 12 balls. Four balls are removed from the second bag. How many balls are left in the second bag?

EXAMPLE

34.75 is . . . 35 to the nearest whole number;   Standard form:
    . . . 34.8 to one decimal place; $561.3 = 5.613 \times 10^2$
    . . . 30 to one significant figure; $56.13 = 5.613 \times 10$
    . . . 34.8 to three significant figures. $5613 = 5.613 \times 10^3$

A Write, to the nearest whole number:

1 7.9
2 4.8
3 3.2
4 17.6
5 48.3
6 58.9
7 104.8
8 83.4
9 156.1
10 2.8
11 208.7
12 8.47
13 3.93
14 27.6
15 54.08
16 130.9
17 29.9
18 64.6
19 687.15
20 300.6

B Write, to 1 place of decimals:

1 5.64
2 5.67
3 43.72
4 5.56
5 4.07
6 18.36
7 224.66
8 37.47
9 11.09
10 100.26
11 3.732
12 3.739
13 5.645
14 30.782
15 46.549
16 3.785
17 4.697
18 0.198
19 3.119
20 16.208

C Write, to 2 significant figures:

1 83.6
2 836.1
3 794.4
4 866
5 4375
6 8580
7 97.09
8 50.72
9 67.8
10 51.93

Write, to 3 significant figures:

11 135.9
12 135.09
13 24.38
14 5.646
15 14.927
16 26.092
17 151.64
18 349.8
19 0.473
20 5.826

D Write, to the nearest hundred:

1 459.3
2 1609
3 325.8
4 680.9
5 7382
6 6579
7 84.5
8 1893.4
9 46.7
10 97.8

Write, to the nearest ten:

11 67.1
12 9.8
13 509
14 156.7
15 529.7
16 486.7
17 75.4
18 568
19 5.9
20 4.2

Write in standard form:

21 140
22 370.1
23 56
24 4912
25 5670
26 74560
27 383.14
28 954
29 954.2
30 954.27

2 decimals

EXAMPLE

32.3	24.5	3.7	$6.15 \times 4 = 24.60 = 24.6$
+ 0.4	− 5.3	−2.45	$15.35 \div 5 = 3.07$
32.7	19.2	1.25	

A
1. $1.2 + 0.4$
2. $2.3 + 0.54$
3. $1.3 + 4.9$
4. $4.7 + 9.9$
5. $0.8 + 3.78$
6. $6.3 - 0.2$
7. $5.6 - 3.4$
8. $4.3 - 2.9$
9. $6.5 - 5.12$
10. $6.7 - 6.3$
11. $3.5 + 43.6$
12. $4.3 + 52.6$
13. $47.9 + 16.6$
14. $48.2 + 6.7$
15. $34.8 + 81.4$
16. $64.9 - 37.4$
17. $47.9 - 16.6$
18. $158.9 - 52.52$
19. $384.5 - 157.3$
20. $659.3 - 84.62$

B
1. 1.4×2
2. 5.7×4
3. 5.3×3
4. 6.32×5
5. 4.51×2
6. $3.6 \div 6$
7. $4.5 \div 8$
8. $12.4 \div 8$
9. $15.6 \div 3$
10. $24.8 \div 4$
11. 56.7×6
12. 48.6×3
13. 3.25×6
14. 67.4×5
15. 14.7×5
16. $46.5 \div 3$
17. $28.8 \div 3$
18. $150.5 \div 5$
19. $816.4 \div 4$
20. $62.3 \div 7$

C
1. Find the sum of 4.3 and 16.4.
2. What is the difference between 11.4 and 6.8?
3. Find the total of 6.3, 5.9 and 0.5.
4. How much more is 12.3 than 5.7?
5. By how much does 74.3 exceed 65?
6. Add together 5.6, 14.2 and 7.08.
7. Find the sum of 67.3 and 28.9.
8. How much less than 100 is 67.8?
9. What is 78.9 to the nearest ten?
10. What is 412.8 to the nearest hundred?
11. Find the product of 200 and 4.7.
12. Multiply 0.61 by 30.
13. Find the number 200 times greater than 0.35.
14. Multiply 5000 by 1.4
15. Find the total of three hundred 4.6s.
16. Find the number 70 times bigger than 0.03.
17. Multiply eight thousand by 6.7.
18. Find the product of nine hundred and 13.4.
19. Which is greater, five thousand or the product of 900 and 1.5?
20. Which is smaller, fourteen thousand or the product of 600 and 2.8?

EXAMPLE

$5.7 \times 10 = 57$	$0.57 \times 10 = 5.7$	$93 \div 10 = 9.3$
$5.7 \times 100 = 570$	$0.57 \times 100 = 57$	$93 \div 100 = 0.93$

A
1 3.5×10
2 3.6×100
3 3.21×10
4 0.35×10
5 0.418×100
6 2.6×20
7 5.31×30
8 6.2×400
9 3.5×30
10 4.3×400
11 4.2×200
12 12.3×20
13 5.31×40
14 62.1×30
15 1.23×400
16 3.51×200
17 0.023×60
18 1.08×300
19 5.02×400
20 0.062×200

B
1 2.35×60
2 57.8×400
3 71.42×20
4 278.3×500
5 38.2×400
6 48.1×700
7 58.2×60
8 478.3×600
9 4.368×50
10 56.7×80
11 527.4×300
12 34.5×400
13 8.09×500
14 6.023×800
15 15.08×500
16 2.4×800
17 2.5×900
18 13.4×50
19 4.05×600
20 0.89×600

C
1 $5.6 \div 10$
2 $35.6 \div 10$
3 $54 \div 20$
4 $450 \div 30$
5 $4.6 \div 20$
6 $6.3 \div 30$
7 $85.6 \div 40$
8 $3.69 \div 300$
9 $784 \div 500$
10 $426 \div 600$
11 $2.46 \div 30$
12 $0.48 \div 50$
13 $4.5 \div 600$
14 $35.6 \div 500$
15 $0.78 \div 60$
16 $560 \div 700$
17 $40.08 \div 50$
18 $6.012 \div 60$
19 $7.228 \div 40$
20 $81.36 \div 900$

D
1 Write in order of size, smallest first, 0.09, 0.191, 0.11.
2 Which is larger, 0.066 or 0.0625?
3 What is the next whole number after 40.99?
4 Write in order of size, smallest first, 0.33, 0.325, 0.099, 0.331.
5 Which is the correct answer for 0.3^2: 0.06, 0.9, 0.09, 0.6?
6 Write down the number 10 more than 16.5.
7 Write down the number 10 less than 11.05.
8 Use the sign $<$ to write a true statement about 10×1.45 and $145 \div 100$.
9 Use the sign $>$ to write a true statement about $10 + 0.9$ and $11 - 1.1$.
10 Which is the square of 0.4: 0.16, 0.8, 0.44, 0.016, 0.08?

EXAMPLE

14.8×309

This is approximately 15×300

$$15 \times 300 = 4500$$

The exact answer is 4573.2

Find an approximate answer and the exact result.
Show the numbers chosen for your approximation.

A
1 12.1×203
2 9.9×304
3 7.8×599
4 19.9×39.4
5 6.03×5.14
6 8.09×401
7 15.99×38.9
8 289×4.01
9 45.9×489
10 3.07×59
11 15.1×780
12 34.6×800
13 86.7×500
14 60.2×378
15 14.9×60.4

B
1 $50.4 \div 2$
2 $50.6 \div 20$
3 $61.8 \div 30$
4 $45.6 \div 400$
5 $98.21 \div 70$
6 $56.08 \div 80$
7 $38.13 \div 41$
8 $725.7 \div 59$
9 $2734.2 \div 42$
10 $363.6 \div 1.01$
11 $4.93 \div 9.86$
12 $48.16 \div 6.02$
13 $719.1 \div 79.9$
14 $59.4 \div 4.95$
15 $780.52 \div 30.02$

C 1 At the football match John and his friend started arguing about the
size of the crowd. His friend said there were more than twenty
thousand. John tried to count the heads. He knew that there were 30
blocks and he thought there were 10 rows in each block. He then
counted the number of heads in one row and said all the rows looked
about the same. There were about 40 in a row.
What would be John's estimate for the size of the crowd?

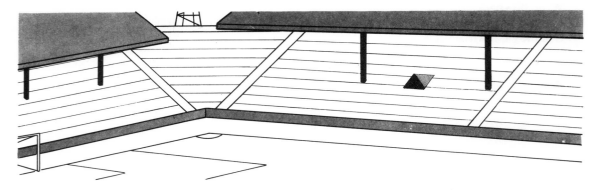

2 When the 4 o'clock train to Birmingham pulled out of the station,
there were no empty seats and a few people were standing in each
coach. There were 7 coaches on the train and no buffet car. Each
coach had 60 seats.
Make a statement about the number of people on that train.

8

EXAMPLE

$$6.7$$
$$\times 0.2$$
$$\overline{1.34}$$

$$15.9 \times 10^2 = 1590$$
$$1.8 \times 10^{-2} = 0.018$$

$$0.48 \div 0.3 = 4.8 \div 3$$
$$= 1.6$$

A
1 4.5×0.3
2 3.4×2.1
3 0.42×0.03
4 0.34×0.2
5 14.2×0.4
6 2.03×0.3
7 21.4×0.4
8 0.023×0.3
9 0.04×0.02
10 0.05×0.3
11 0.24×0.5
12 1.43×0.003
13 4.21×0.5
14 54.2×0.05
15 0.324×0.2
16 0.042×3.1
17 3.02×4.3
18 15.3×0.23
19 0.042×1.4
20 2.45×0.4

B
1 0.36×0.7
2 7.8×0.4
3 5.27×0.3
4 67.5×0.6
5 58.9×0.08
6 632.1×0.06
7 5.32×0.006
8 46.8×0.03
9 6.75×0.4
10 8.94×0.004
11 43.7×1.6
12 6.78×3.7
13 0.089×6.2
14 8.96×1.8
15 56.7×0.94
16 5.9×3.2
17 0.84×0.035
18 5.32×0.63
19 15.8×4.7
20 6.5×0.058

C
1 $0.86 \div 0.2$
2 $0.036 \div 0.3$
3 $0.052 \div 0.4$
4 $0.0206 \div 0.2$
5 $0.0515 \div 0.05$
6 $9.42 \div 0.3$
7 $1.026 \div 0.02$
8 $0.1684 \div 0.004$
9 $1.615 \div .0.05$
10 $0.29 \div 0.02$
11 $0.82 \div 0.2$
12 $0.208 \div 0.04$
13 $0.129 \div 0.03$
14 $0.016 \div 0.005$
15 $9.24 \div 0.4$
16 $0.48 \div 1.2$
17 $6.9 \div 2.3$
18 $0.624 \div 0.12$
19 $0.123 \div 0.41$
20 $117.3 \div 2.3$

D
1 1.7×10^2
2 2.5×10^3
3 3.1×10^2
4 5.6×10^3
5 4.7×10^2
6 25.8×10^3
7 56.3×10^4
8 38.1×10^2
9 49.6×10^3
10 11.2×10^2

11 0.15×10^2
12 0.23×10^3
13 0.46×10^2
14 0.85×10
15 0.87×10^2
16 0.95×10^3
17 0.73×10^3
18 0.61×10
19 0.84×10
20 0.98×10^2

21 1.8×10^{-1}
22 2.4×10^{-2}
23 3.1×10^{-1}
24 3.2×10^{-2}
25 4.5×10^{-1}
26 16.9×10^{-3}
27 34.8×10^{-2}
28 28.1×10^{-1}
29 49.4×10^{-2}
30 69.3×10^{-1}

EXAMPLE
$4.82 \div 20 = 0.482 \div 2 = 0.241$
$3240 \div 400 = 32.4 \div 4 = 8.1$

A
1. $4.62 \div 20$
2. $9.63 \div 30$
3. $84.8 \div 40$
4. $690.3 \div 30$
5. $86.4 \div 200$
6. $872.8 \div 200$
7. $650.5 \div 500$
8. $92.48 \div 400$
9. $75.9 \div 30$
10. $968.4 \div 400$
11. $6.505 \div 50$
12. $755.5 \div 500$
13. $460.8 \div 400$
14. $75.09 \div 30$
15. $56.8 \div 400$
16. $906.3 \div 300$
17. $1565 \div 500$
18. $6080.4 \div 40$
19. $45.75 \div 30$
20. $860.4 \div 400$

B
1. $2160 \div 600$
2. $12\,810 \div 700$
3. $194.4 \div 80$
4. $810 \div 900$
5. $8960 \div 800$
6. $72 \div 600$
7. $2.24 \div 40$
8. $950 \div 500$
9. $180 \div 600$
10. $513 \div 90$
11. $3150 \div 500$
12. $774 \div 900$
13. $5.6 \div 80$
14. $1170 \div 600$
15. $1435 \div 50$
16. $3892 \div 40$
17. $1971 \div 300$
18. $47\,070 \div 900$
19. $41.5 \div 50$
20. $3.55 \div 50$

C
1. $0.21 \div 70$
2. $4560 \div 800$
3. $24.3 \div 90$
4. $34.8 \div 600$
5. $1404.9 \div 700$
6. $7.2 \div 900$
7. $4002.4 \div 80$
8. $3432.8 \div 700$
9. $1.95 \div 500$
10. $3606 \div 60$

Give the answers correct to 1 decimal place:
11. $640 \div 30$
12. $570 \div 700$
13. $894 \div 90$
14. $95.7 \div 300$
15. $5720 \div 90$
16. $46 \div 700$
17. $80 \div 900$
18. $74.2 \div 30$
19. $512 \div 90$
20. $4525 \div 700$

D
1. Find one twentieth of 4.7.
2. Divide seven hundred and three by 500.
3. Find one seven hundredth of 31.5.
4. What must 90 be multiplied by to give 7.2?
5. Find the product of one six hundredth and 25 380.
6. Divide one thousand and thirty-five by 90.
7. Find one fiftieth of 0.06.
8. Divide 6.78 by three hundred.
9. What must 70 be multiplied by to give 371?
10. How many 30s in 75?

3 number applications

ROMAN NUMERALS

A These are the Roman numerals up to 30.

1 I	**7** VII	**13** XIII	**19** XIX	**25** XXV
2 II	**8** VIII	**14** XIV	**20** XX	**26** XXVI
3 III	**9** IX	**15** XV	**21** XXI	**27** XXVII
4 IV	**10** X	**16** XVI	**22** XXII	**28** XXVIII
5 V	**11** XI	**17** XVII	**23** XXIII	**29** XXIX
6 VI	**12** XII	**18** XVIII	**24** XXIV	**30** XXX

Two matches can make the numerals:

Three matches can make:

1 Which numerals up to XXX need four matches?

2 Which numerals need five matches?

3 Which numerals need six matches?

4 Which numerals need seven matches?

5 Which numerals need eight matches?

PATTERNS WITH MATCHES

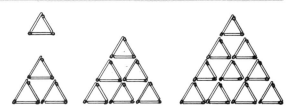

B 1 Draw the block of 4 triangles, counting the number of extra matches as you draw. Enter the numbers in the table.

Number of matches on one side	1	2	3	4		
Number of triangles	1	4				
Number of matches	3	9				
Number of extra matches	0	6				

2 Draw the next block of triangles by adding extra matches you need to make the next row of triangles. Enter the results in the table.

3 What pattern do you see in the numbers of triangles?

4 If you had drawn the triangle with 10 matches on each side, how many small triangles would there be?

How many triangles would there be if there were 20 matches on each side?

5 The number of matches used is a multiple of 3. Try dividing these numbers by 3, and what sequence of numbers is produced?

6 What pattern can you find in the number of extra matches used?

NUMBERS IN USE

A There are numbers on many things round about us. The number has been left off this diary:

   1 Which number in this list should be on the diary?
     7,   1973,   30,   1,   33⅓.

   The missing numbers for all these things are in this list.

Write down which number belongs to which thing.

B These are the numbers missing from the things below:
   .033,   324,   150,   10,   8 . . . 3,   20,   7′ 6″.

   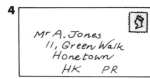

  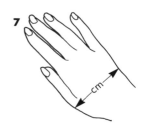

Make a list to show where they belong.

C Use these numbers in the following sentences:
   31,   360,   13,   6,   200,   80.

   1 I wear size . . . shoes.
   2 The table is . . . cm high.
   3 There are . . . days in January.
   4 There are . . . minutes in six hours.
   5 There are . . . school days in a year.
   6 A baker's dozen is . . .

STEPS

A

1 How many hops from ▷ to ⊨ ?
2 How many hops from ⊨ to ⊐ ?

B

```
|—+—+—+—+—+—+—+—+—|
      3           8        11
```

1 How many hops from 3 to 8?
2 How many hops from 3 to 11?

C ▷1 ▷2 ▷3 ▷4 ▷5 ▷6 ▷7 ▷8 ▷9

1 Flags numbered 3 to 7 are removed. How many flags are removed? Count them.

2 Put all the flags back. Flags numbered 2 to 5 are coloured. How many are coloured?

D 1 2 3 4 5 6 7 8 9 10 11 12 13 14 15

1 Boxes numbered 3 to 6 have lids. How many have lids? How many do not have lids?
2 Balls are put into boxes numbered 7 to 11. How many boxes have balls in them?
3 Boxes numbered 8 to 13 are painted blue. How many boxes are blue?

E Imagine you are walking along this road. House numbers 1, 3, 5, are on your left.
The first five houses on your left have blue doors.

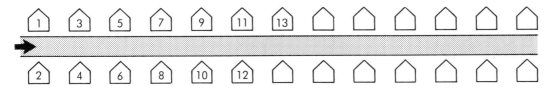

1 What is the number of the third blue house?
2 What is the number of the last blue house?

The first four houses on your right have green doors.

3 What is the number of the first green door?
4 What is the number of the last green door?

5 There are twenty houses on your right. What is the number of the last one?

The last number on your left is 39.

6 How many houses are there in the road?
7 How many houses are there on your left?

F

```
←——————————————————————————————→
 -5  -4  -3  -2  -1  0  1  2  3  4  5  6  7  8  9  10
-                                                      +
```

1 How far is −1 from +2?
2 How far is +4 from −3?
3 How many steps between −3 and 0?

4 How far is −5 from +5?
5 Which point is 7 steps up the numberline from −5?

MACHINES FOR EQUATIONS

A When 2 goes into this machine, check that it becomes 12, 21, 7. Answer 7 comes out.

Write down what comes out when these numbers are put into the machine:
1 1 **2** 5 **3** 3 **4** 10 **5** 6 **6** x **7** y

B

Write down what comes out when these are put into the machine:
1 3 **2** 7 **3** 5 **4** 11 **5** 9 **6** x **7** y

C

Write down what comes out when these are put into the machine:
1 10 **2** 16 **3** 12 **4** 8 **5** 20 **6** x **7** y

D

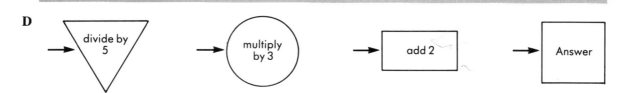

Write down what comes out when these are put into the machine:
1 15 **2** 25 **3** 45 **4** 5 **5** 60 **6** x **7** y

E 1 Draw a machine to show $2x + 3$.
If 4 is put into this machine, what comes out?

2 Draw a machine to show $3x + 4 = 10$.
What is put into it to make 10 come out?

14

CROSS NUMBER

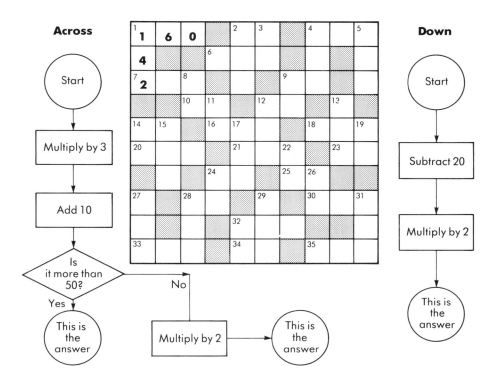

15

Across

Put these numbers into the 'across' machine.

1 50	**20** 200
2 6	**21** 151
4 45	**23** 8
6 36	**24** 16
7 72	**25** 7
9 10	**28** 12
10 8	**30** 85
12 4	**32** 60
14 21	**33** 84
16 71	**34** 11
18 81	**35** 42

Down

Put these numbers into the 'down' machine.

1 91	**15** 178
2 279	**17** 144
3 54	**19** 39
4 70	**22** 38
5 270	**24** 46
8 53	**26** 31
9 62	**27** 81
11 61	**28** 476
12 238	**29** 168
13 198	**31** 283
14 58	

NUMBER MISCELLANY – I wonder if it continues?

1 $7 \times 7 =$
 $67 \times 67 =$
 $667 \times 667 =$
 $6667 \times 6667 =$

6 $9 \times 6 =$
 $99 \times 66 =$
 $999 \times 666 =$

7 $1^2 =$
 $11^2 =$
 $111^2 =$

2 $1 \times 8 - 1 =$
 $21 \times 8 - 1 =$
 $321 \times 8 - 1 =$

8 $1 \times 9 = 10 - ?$
 $2 \times 9 = 20 - ?$
 $3 \times 9 = 30 - ?$

3 $1 \times 9 - 1 =$
 $21 \times 9 - 1 =$
 $321 \times 9 - 1 =$

9 $1 \times 8 = 10 - ?$
 $2 \times 8 = 20 - ?$
 $3 \times 8 = 30 - ?$

4 $0 \times 9 + 1 =$
 $1 \times 9 + 2 =$
 $12 \times 9 + 3 =$
 $123 \times 9 + 4 =$

10 $1^3 = 1$
 $1^3 + 2^3 = 9 = 3^2$
 $1^3 + 2^3 + 3^3 =$

5 $1 \times 999 =$
 $2 \times 999 =$
 $3 \times 999 =$
 $4 \times 999 =$
 $5 \times 999 =$

4 fractions

EXAMPLE

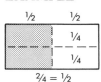

½ ½
¼
¼

²⁄₄ = ½

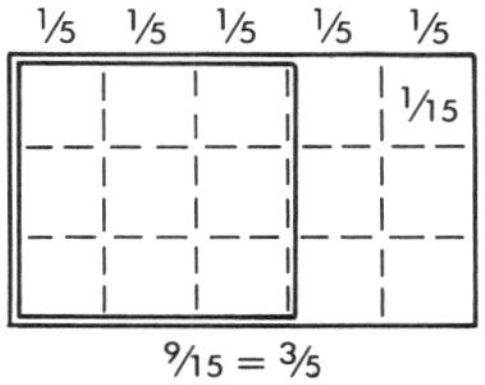

⅕ ⅕ ⅕ ⅕ ⅕
¹⁄₁₅

⁹⁄₁₅ = ³⁄₅

Using a calculator:

$\frac{2}{5} = 2 \div 5 = 0.4$

$\frac{3}{8} = 3 \div 8 = 0.375$

A Complete:

1 $\frac{1}{2} = \frac{}{4}$

2 $\frac{1}{2} = \frac{}{6}$

3 $\frac{1}{2} = \frac{}{8}$

4 $\frac{1}{2} = \frac{}{10}$

5 $\frac{1}{4} = \frac{}{8}$

6 $\frac{1}{4} = \frac{}{12}$

7 $\frac{1}{4} = \frac{}{20}$

8 $\frac{3}{4} = \frac{}{8}$

9 $\frac{3}{4} = \frac{}{12}$

10 $\frac{3}{4} = \frac{}{20}$

11 $\frac{1}{6} = \frac{}{12}$

12 $\frac{1}{6} = \frac{}{18}$

13 $\frac{1}{6} = \frac{}{30}$

14 $\frac{5}{6} = \frac{}{12}$

15 $\frac{5}{6} = \frac{}{24}$

16 $\frac{1}{5} = \frac{}{10}$

17 $\frac{1}{5} = \frac{}{20}$

18 $\frac{1}{5} = \frac{}{25}$

19 $\frac{1}{5} = \frac{}{15}$

20 $\frac{1}{5} = \frac{}{40}$

B Complete:

1 $\frac{1}{2} = \frac{}{100}$

2 $\frac{1}{8} = \frac{}{16}$

3 $\frac{3}{8} = \frac{}{16}$

4 $\frac{5}{8} = \frac{}{16}$

5 $\frac{3}{10} = \frac{}{100}$

6 $\frac{7}{10} = \frac{}{100}$

7 $\frac{3}{10} = \frac{}{30}$

8 $\frac{5}{9} = \frac{}{18}$

9 $\frac{7}{9} = \frac{}{18}$

10 $\frac{5}{12} = \frac{}{24}$

11 $\frac{7}{12} = \frac{}{24}$

12 $\frac{11}{12} = \frac{}{36}$

13 $\frac{5}{12} = \frac{}{48}$

14 $\frac{7}{15} = \frac{}{30}$

15 $\frac{1}{20} = \frac{}{40}$

16 $\frac{3}{20} = \frac{}{60}$

17 $\frac{3}{20} = \frac{}{100}$

18 $\frac{7}{50} = \frac{}{100}$

19 $\frac{11}{20} = \frac{}{100}$

20 $\frac{13}{50} = \frac{}{100}$

C Use a calculator to express as a decimal:

1 $\frac{1}{2}$

2 $\frac{1}{4}$

3 $\frac{3}{4}$

4 $\frac{1}{5}$

5 $\frac{3}{5}$

6 $\frac{2}{5}$

7 $\frac{3}{10}$

8 $\frac{1}{15}$

9 $\frac{7}{15}$

10 $\frac{1}{40}$

11 $\frac{21}{40}$

12 $\frac{3}{8}$

13 $\frac{5}{12}$

14 $\frac{1}{3}$

15 $\frac{1}{6}$

16 $\frac{4}{9}$

17 $\frac{2}{3}$

18 $\frac{17}{40}$

19 $\frac{13}{20}$

20 $\frac{13}{40}$

D What fraction of each shape has been shaded?

1
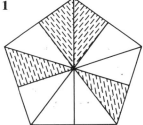

2
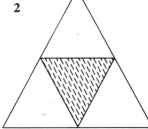

3

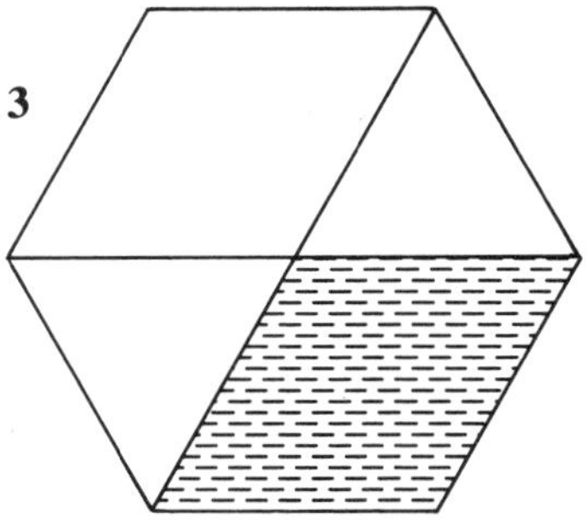

EXAMPLE

$\frac{1}{2} + \frac{1}{2} = 1$ whole

$\frac{1}{3} + \frac{1}{3} + \frac{1}{3} = 1$ whole

$\frac{1}{4} + \frac{3}{4} = 1$ whole

$\frac{1}{2} = \frac{2}{4}$

$\frac{1}{2} + \frac{1}{4} = \frac{3}{4}$

$\frac{1}{2} + \frac{1}{4} + \frac{3}{4} = \frac{6}{4} = 1\frac{1}{2}$

$\frac{1}{2} + \frac{1}{3} = \frac{3}{6} + \frac{2}{6} = \frac{5}{6}$

$\frac{1}{2} + \frac{3}{4} + \frac{1}{3} = \frac{6}{12} + \frac{9}{12} + \frac{4}{12} = \frac{19}{12}$

$= 1\frac{7}{12}$

$6\frac{2}{5} - 2\frac{5}{8} = 4\frac{16 - 25}{40} = 3\frac{31}{40}$

A
1. $\frac{1}{2} + \frac{1}{2}$
2. $\frac{1}{3} + \frac{1}{3}$
3. $\frac{1}{5} + \frac{1}{5}$
4. $\frac{2}{5} + \frac{1}{5}$
5. $\frac{3}{5} + \frac{1}{5}$
6. $1\frac{1}{2} + 1\frac{1}{2}$
7. $2\frac{1}{3} + 2\frac{1}{3}$
8. $3\frac{1}{5} + 3\frac{1}{5}$
9. $4\frac{1}{2} + 4\frac{1}{2}$
10. $3\frac{2}{5} + 1\frac{1}{5}$
11. $\frac{3}{5} - \frac{2}{5}$
12. $\frac{2}{3} - \frac{1}{3}$
13. $\frac{4}{5} - \frac{1}{5}$
14. $3\frac{2}{5} - 2\frac{1}{5}$
15. $4\frac{4}{5} - 1\frac{2}{5}$
16. $2\frac{3}{4} - 1\frac{1}{4}$
17. $5\frac{3}{4} - 2\frac{1}{2}$
18. $5\frac{1}{2} - 2\frac{1}{4}$
19. $5\frac{2}{3} - 3\frac{1}{3}$
20. $4\frac{3}{4} - 2\frac{1}{4}$

B
1. $\frac{1}{3} + \frac{1}{2}$
2. $\frac{1}{4} + \frac{1}{5}$
3. $\frac{1}{3} + \frac{1}{5}$
4. $\frac{1}{5} + \frac{1}{7}$
5. $\frac{1}{9} + \frac{1}{8}$
6. $\frac{1}{4} + \frac{3}{7}$
7. $2\frac{1}{4} + 1\frac{1}{5}$
8. $3\frac{1}{2} + 2\frac{1}{3}$
9. $4\frac{2}{5} + 3\frac{1}{3}$
10. $7\frac{1}{5} + 5\frac{1}{8}$
11. $2\frac{1}{5} - 1\frac{1}{8}$
12. $2\frac{2}{3} - 1\frac{1}{4}$
13. $5\frac{1}{4} - 2\frac{1}{5}$
14. $7\frac{2}{3} - 2\frac{2}{7}$
15. $6\frac{5}{7} - 3\frac{1}{8}$
16. $9\frac{2}{5} - 2\frac{1}{9}$
17. $8\frac{3}{7} - 5\frac{3}{8}$
18. $6\frac{2}{3} - 2\frac{2}{7}$
19. $9\frac{3}{4} - 3\frac{2}{9}$
20. $8\frac{3}{4} - 2\frac{5}{8}$

C
1. $3\frac{3}{4} + 2\frac{3}{5}$
2. $4\frac{1}{3} + 2\frac{6}{7}$
3. $3\frac{2}{3} + 4\frac{8}{9}$
4. $4\frac{4}{5} + 7\frac{7}{10}$
5. $9\frac{9}{10} + 6\frac{2}{3}$
6. $2\frac{2}{3} + 3\frac{4}{5}$
7. $5\frac{3}{4} + 2\frac{7}{9}$
8. $7\frac{3}{5} + 2\frac{8}{9}$
9. $8\frac{3}{5} + 2\frac{1}{4}$
10. $9\frac{5}{8} + 2\frac{6}{7}$
11. $4\frac{7}{8} - 2\frac{1}{2}$
12. $3\frac{1}{3} - 1\frac{5}{6}$
13. $8\frac{7}{9} - 1\frac{11}{12}$
14. $7\frac{1}{4} - 2\frac{6}{7}$
15. $12\frac{1}{4} - 7\frac{8}{9}$
16. $5\frac{1}{3} - 2\frac{4}{5}$
17. $6\frac{3}{4} - 2\frac{9}{10}$
18. $9\frac{3}{8} - 2\frac{7}{9}$
19. $12\frac{2}{5} - 3\frac{7}{8}$
20. $12\frac{3}{4} - 6\frac{4}{7}$

D

1. Mrs Jones's salary is £7500. When she retires in two months time, she will get a pension which is $\frac{2}{5}$ of this salary. How much is her annual pension?

2. When a certain ball is dropped it bounces up to $\frac{7}{10}$ of the height from which it was dropped. To what height will it rise when dropped from a height of 300 cm
   (a) after the first bounce?
   (b) after the second bounce?
   (c) after how many bounces will it rise less than 50 cm?

3. A 15 litre container is full of liquid. How many $1\frac{1}{2}$ litre bottles can be filled with this liquid?

4. I normally use half a ton of coal a week. How long can I expect $3\frac{1}{2}$ tons to last?

5. A car has been travelling at a steady speed for $\frac{3}{4}$ of an hour and the driver notices that he has done 60 km. If the roads remain clear so that he can continue in the same way, how far can he expect to have travelled in the next $1\frac{1}{2}$ hours?

$\frac{3}{4} \times 4 = \frac{3}{4} \times \frac{4}{1}$

$\frac{6}{17} \div 2 = \frac{6}{17} \times \frac{1}{2}$

$3 \times \frac{1}{3} = 1$ whole

$\qquad = 3$

$\qquad = \frac{3}{17}$

$3 \times 2\frac{1}{3} = 6 + 1 = 7$

A
1. $\frac{1}{2} \times 2$
2. $\frac{1}{3} \times 3$
3. $\frac{1}{4} \times 4$
4. $\frac{1}{5} \times 5$
5. $\frac{1}{6} \times 6$
6. $\frac{2}{3} \times 3$
7. $\frac{3}{4} \times 4$
8. $\frac{2}{5} \times 5$
9. $\frac{3}{5} \times 5$
10. $\frac{4}{5} \times 5$
11. $1\frac{1}{2} \times 2$
12. $2\frac{1}{2} \times 2$
13. $3\frac{1}{2} \times 2$
14. $5\frac{1}{2} \times 2$
15. $4\frac{1}{2} \times 2$
16. $3\frac{1}{3} \times 3$
17. $5\frac{1}{3} \times 3$
18. $4\frac{1}{3} \times 3$
19. $5\frac{1}{5} \times 5$
20. $5\frac{1}{4} \times 4$

B
1. $\frac{1}{3} \times 6$
2. $\frac{4}{5} \times 10$
3. $\frac{2}{3} \times 6$
4. $\frac{3}{5} \times 10$
5. $\frac{2}{5} \times 10$
6. $\frac{1}{5} \times 10$
7. $\frac{3}{4} \times 8$
8. $\frac{5}{7} \times 7$
9. $\frac{5}{7} \times 14$
10. $\frac{6}{7} \times 21$
11. $\frac{3}{8} \times 8$
12. $\frac{3}{8} \times 16$
13. $\frac{7}{9} \times 18$
14. $\frac{4}{11} \times 11$
15. $\frac{4}{11} \times 22$
16. $\frac{2}{5} \times 10$
17. $\frac{4}{9} \times 9$
18. $\frac{4}{9} \times 18$
19. $\frac{7}{12} \times 36$
20. $\frac{8}{13} \times 39$

C
1. $\frac{4}{7} \div 2$
2. $\frac{6}{7} \div 2$
3. $\frac{4}{9} \div 2$
4. $\frac{6}{7} \div 3$
5. $\frac{4}{9} \div 4$
6. $\frac{8}{9} \div 2$
7. $\frac{8}{9} \div 4$
8. $\frac{8}{15} \div 2$
9. $\frac{8}{15} \div 4$
10. $\frac{9}{10} \div 3$
11. $2\frac{1}{5} \times 5$
12. $2\frac{2}{5} \times 5$
13. $2\frac{3}{15} \times 5$
14. $3\frac{1}{5} \times 5$
15. $4\frac{1}{5} \times 5$
16. $4\frac{2}{5} \times 5$
17. $4\frac{3}{5} \times 5$
18. $3\frac{3}{4} \times 2$
19. $3\frac{3}{4} \times 4$
20. $4\frac{3}{4} \times 4$

D What fraction of each shape has been left unshaded?

1.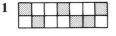

2.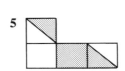

3.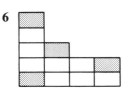

4.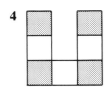

5.

6.

5 percentages

EXAMPLE

The whole square contains 100 tiny squares.
Each tiny square is $\frac{1}{100}$ of the whole square.
$\frac{1}{100} = 0.01$, $1\% = \frac{1}{100} = 0.01$
The strip of 10 squares is $\frac{1}{10}$ of the whole, $\frac{1}{10} = 0.1 = 10\%$.

A Copy and complete:

1

Shaded	Unshaded
$\frac{1}{10}$	$\frac{}{100}$
10%	%
0.1	

5

Shaded	Unshaded
$\frac{25}{100}$	$\frac{}{100}$
	75%
	0.75

2

$\frac{3}{10}$	
30%	
0.3	

6

$\frac{}{20}$	$\frac{}{100}$
%	%
0.05	

3

$\frac{1}{2}$	$\frac{}{100}$
%	%
0.5	

7

$\frac{}{100}$	$\frac{}{100}$
%	%
0.07	

4

$\frac{3}{20}$	$\frac{}{100}$
%	%
0.15	

8

$\frac{2}{5}$	$\frac{}{100}$
%	%
0.4	

B Copy and complete this table of equivalents:

Fraction	$\frac{10}{100}$	$\frac{20}{100}$	$\frac{1}{5}$	$\frac{30}{100}$	$\frac{60}{100}$	$\frac{75}{100}$	$\frac{25}{100}$	$\frac{1}{4}$	$\frac{1}{3}$	$\frac{2}{3}$
Decimal										
Percentage										

C Express as a percentage:

1 0.5	**6** 0.4	**11** 0.6	**16** 0.95
2 0.25	**7** 0.45	**12** 0.3	**17** 0.64
3 0.75	**8** 0.37	**13** 0.9	**18** 0.87
4 1.0	**9** 0.57	**14** 0.8	**19** 0.24
5 0.2	**10** 0.82	**15** 0.7	**20** 0.72

D Express as a decimal

1 20%	**6** 45%	**11** $33\frac{1}{3}\%$	**16** 72%
2 40%	**7** 15%	**12** 90%	**17** 86%
3 60%	**8** 6%	**13** 10%	**18** 35%
4 75%	**9** $12\frac{1}{2}\%$	**14** 7%	**19** 50%
5 25%	**10** 47%	**15** 95%	**20** 53%

EXAMPLE

Full marks are 100% $\frac{6}{12} = \frac{1}{2} = 50\%$ $\frac{20}{30} = \frac{2}{3} = 66\frac{2}{3}\%$

$100\% = \frac{100}{100} = 1$ whole $\frac{15}{20} = \frac{3}{4} = 75\%$ $\frac{30}{80} = \frac{3}{8} = 37\frac{1}{2}\%$

Express the following as percentages:

A
1. $\frac{1}{2}$
2. $\frac{1}{4}$
3. $\frac{3}{4}$
4. $\frac{1}{5}$
5. $\frac{2}{5}$
6. $\frac{3}{5}$
7. $\frac{4}{5}$
8. $\frac{1}{3}$
9. $\frac{2}{3}$
10. $\frac{1}{10}$
11. $\frac{3}{10}$
12. $\frac{7}{10}$
13. $\frac{9}{10}$
14. $\frac{1}{20}$
15. $\frac{1}{40}$
16. $\frac{1}{80}$
17. $\frac{7}{80}$
18. $\frac{5}{80}$
19. $\frac{3}{80}$
20. $\frac{3}{16}$

B
1. 2 out of 4
2. 4 out of 8
3. 3 out of 6
4. 1 out of 4
5. 1 out of 5
6. 2 out of 5
7. 3 out of 5
8. 4 out of 40
9. 4 out of 12
10. 5 out of 15
11. 5 out of 25
12. 2 out of 10
13. 5 out of 20
14. 3 out of 12
15. 2 out of 6
16. 30 out of 40
17. 4 out of 5
18. 6 out of 24
19. 4 out of 20
20. 5 out of 10

C
1. 6 out of 8
2. 30 out of 50
3. 20 out of 50
4. 12 out of 20
5. 12 out of 15
6. 28 out of 35
7. 24 out of 30
8. 3 out of 10
9. 36 out of 48
10. 14 out of 20
11. 27 out of 30
12. 35 out of 50
13. 18 out of 20
14. 16 out of 20
15. 45 out of 50
16. 20 out of 160
17. 15 out of 24
18. 15 out of 40
19. 28 out of 32
20. 25 out of 40

D A large scale survey was made of the canned foods used in three different regions. The results were displayed in pie charts. There is a serious mistake in one set of figures. Which is it and how is it recognised?

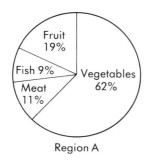

Region A

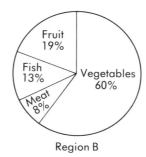

Region B

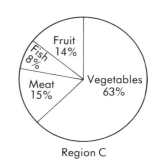

Region C

21

EXAMPLE

$50\% = \frac{50}{100} = \frac{1}{2}$	$10\% = \frac{1}{10}$	$90\% = \frac{9}{10}$	$33\frac{1}{3}\% = \frac{1}{3}$	$1\% = \frac{1}{100} = 0.01$
$25\% = \frac{25}{100} = \frac{1}{4}$	$30\% = \frac{3}{10}$	$20\% = \frac{1}{5}$	$5\% = \frac{1}{20}$	$7\% = \frac{7}{100} = 0.07$
$75\% = \frac{75}{100} = \frac{3}{4}$	$70\% = \frac{7}{10}$	$40\% = \frac{2}{5}$	$12\frac{1}{2}\% = \frac{1}{8}$	$15\% = \frac{15}{100} = 0.15$

Find the values of:

A
1 50% of 12
2 50% of 30
3 50% of 24
4 25% of 24
5 25% of 20
6 25% of 28
7 25% of 32
8 50% of 32
9 50% of 26
10 50% of 44
11 25% of 44
12 $33\frac{1}{3}$% of 36
13 $33\frac{1}{3}$% of 39
14 $33\frac{1}{3}$% of 42
15 $33\frac{1}{3}$% of 63
16 25% of 56
17 25% of 48
18 25% of 120
19 $33\frac{1}{3}$% of 48
20 20% of 35

B
1 20% of 45
2 20% of 40
3 20% of 60
4 20% of 55
5 20% of 85
6 75% of 20
7 75% of 24
8 75% of 48
9 75% of 32
10 40% of 50
11 40% of 65
12 40% of 75
13 40% of 90
14 60% of 65
15 60% of 85
16 80% of 95
17 80% of 75
18 30% of 95
19 60% of 110
20 40% of 120

C
1 30% of 85p
2 70% of 75p
3 90% of 55p
4 60% of £200
5 80% of £300
6 90% of £2000
7 $12\frac{1}{2}$% of £4000
8 $62\frac{1}{2}$% of £6000
9 $37\frac{1}{2}$% of £12 000
10 $87\frac{1}{2}$% of £14 000

If VAT is payable at 15%, find the VAT on:

11 £30
12 £50
13 £120
14 £36
15 £3.60
16 £4.80
17 £5.60
18 £8.40
19 £12.40
20 £36.80

D
1 Out of a class of 30 pupils 20% were absent. How many were present?

2 A sale notice said '10% off marked price'. How much would you pay for an article marked at £35?

3 A new car cost £4400. In the first year it depreciated by 25%. How much was it worth at the end of the first year?

4 In a sale, a coat originally marked at £250 was reduced by 20%. What was the new price?

5 VAT at 15% was added to a bill of £16. What was the total cost?

6 Production at a factory making 250 cars a day rose by 8%. How many cars will now be produced each day?

7 The number of unemployed was 2 400 000. If it fell by 10% what would be the new total?

8 Which is greater and by how much: 75% of £600 or 60% of £750?

For each shape write down:

(a) the fraction of the whole which has been shaded.

(b) the % of the whole which has been shaded.

(c) the % of the whole which has been left unshaded.

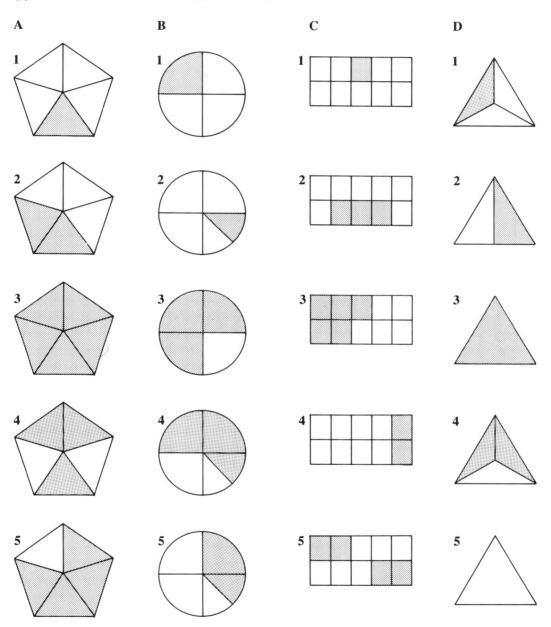

EXAMPLE

A shopkeeper has paid £70 for goods. He wants 50% profit on his cost.
50% of £70 = £35.
The customer has to pay £70 + £35 = £105.

The simple interest on £65 at 10% per annum is 10% of £65 = £6.50.
The simple interest on £65 at 10% for 2 years is 2 × £6.50 = £13.00.

A Calculate the price to be paid:

Cost price	Profit
1 £60	50%
2 £40	50%
3 £50	10%
4 £50	20%
5 £100	20%
6 £30	20%
7 £80	25%
8 £160	25%
9 £200	25%
10 £60	$33\frac{1}{3}$%

Marked price	Reduction
11 £16	$12\frac{1}{2}$%
12 £20	20%
13 £36	25%
14 £40	10%
15 £36	50%
16 £60	5%
17 £80	20%
18 £400	$12\frac{1}{2}$%
19 £720	$33\frac{1}{3}$%
20 £700	40%

B Calculate the simple interest for 1 year on:

1 £40 at 10%
2 £30 at 10%
3 £50 at 10%
4 £60 at 10%
5 £40 at 8%
6 £50 at 6%
7 £60 at 6%
8 £40 at 9%
9 £50 at 8%
10 £60 at 8%

Calculate the simple interest on:

11 £700 at 9% for 2 years
12 £900 at 7% for 3 years
13 £800 at 8% for 2 years
14 £500 at 9% for 4 years
15 £700 at 8% for 2 years
16 £800 at 6% for 3 years
17 £900 at 9% for 4 years
18 £700 at 7% for 3 years
19 £800 at 9% for 2 years
20 £850 at 10% for 4 years

C **1** Jane was told by a car salesman that if she bought a new car, its value by the end of its first year would have depreciated by 20%. During the second year the value depreciates by only 15% of its value at the beginning of the second year. Jane chose a car costing £8000.

(a) How much could she expect it to depreciate in the first year?
(b) How much would it be worth at the beginning of the second year?
(c) How much should she expect it to be worth at the end of 2 years?
(d) Express the price expected at the end of the first two years as a percentage of the purchase price.

To buy on hire purchase, a deposit of 20% of the cash price had to be paid. The balance is paid in 24 monthly equal instalments of £320.

(e) How much was this deposit?
(f) How much would she have to pay for the car altogether?

2 The cash price of a TV set is £350. The HP terms are 10% deposit and 12 equal instalments of £32.65.

(a) How much is needed for the deposit?
(b) How much is paid over the year for the instalments?
(c) How much extra is paid for using HP?

24

EXAMPLE
20% of £35 = 0.2 × £35 = £7

A Increase the following by 10%:

1 £100

2 £350

3 £480

4 £940

5 £820

6 £670

7 £210

8 £780

9 £360

10 £230

11 £684

12 £335

13 £762

14 £875

15 £106

B Increase the following:

1 £100 by 25%

2 £350 by 20%

3 £480 by $33\frac{1}{3}$%

4 £840 by $12\frac{1}{2}$%

5 £400 by $37\frac{1}{2}$%

6 £250 by 20%

7 £320 by $62\frac{1}{2}$%

8 £3.60 by 20%

9 £3.60 by 40%

10 £3.60 by 60%

11 £160 by 40%

12 £160 by 60%

13 £160 by 80%

14 £564 by $37\frac{1}{2}$%

15 £428 by $12\frac{1}{2}$%

C Decrease the following:

1 £200 by 25%

2 £450 by 20%

3 £840 by $12\frac{1}{2}$%

4 £880 by $37\frac{1}{2}$%

5 £240 by $87\frac{1}{2}$%

6 £65.65 by 20%

7 £72.40 by 25%

8 £84.84 by 25%

9 £96.50 by 20%

10 £75.50 by 5%

11 £84.48 by $33\frac{1}{3}$%

12 £35.20 by 5%

13 £167.50 by 20%

14 £14.60 by $2\frac{1}{2}$%

15 £21 000 by $12\frac{1}{2}$%

D 1 A house was valued at £45 000.
2 years later, the value was £48 000.
What was the percentage increase?

2 The average weekly wage of a man rose
from £60 to £65.
What was the percentage increase?

3 A town's population was 20 000 and it
then fell by 10%. What is the population
now?

4 A refrigerator was sold for £80, giving the
retailer a profit of £20.
What was his percentage profit?

5 A personal stereo is advertised as costing
£25 plus VAT at 15%.
What is the total cost of this stereo?

6 A carpet in a shop display is marked
£600. The shop allows a discount of 5%
for cash. How much is this discount
worth?

7 The normal price of a jacket is £30. In the
sale, it is marked down to £24.
(a) How much has the price been
reduced?
(b) Find the percentage reduction on the
normal price.

8 Carl got 8 out of 10 on a Maths test. At
the end of the month he scored 51 out of
60 on a longer test.
Write both scores as percentages.
In which test did he do better?

6 money

EXAMPLE

£304.60 + 32p	304.60	£201.06 − £23.46	201.06
	+ 0.32		− 23.46
=£304.92	304.92	=£177.60	177.60

A 1 £1.20 + 34p
2 £6.12 + 34p
3 £2.20 + 42p
4 £32.54 + £1.23
5 £6.23 + £1
6 £34.10 + £5.25
7 £2.35 + £16.32
8 £4.50 + £2.60
9 £6.32 + £5.30
10 £3.21 + £40.64
11 £5.60 − 35p
12 £30.84 − 33p
13 £23.45 − £1.44
14 £56.70 − £24.55
15 £75.20 − £4.60
16 £6.54 − £1.32
17 £8.96 − £3.64
18 £70.09 − £7
19 £46.60 − £24.55
20 £64.50 − £1.34

B 1 £37.80 + 68p
2 £3.78 + £60.09
3 £20.08 + £9.10
4 £609.10 + £307.06
5 £400.02 + £7.99
6 £45.67 + £4.78
7 £58.90 + £7
8 89p + £6.70
9 56p + £48.80
10 £608.38 + £87.86
11 £600.30 − £60.03
12 £501.87 − £35.69
13 £603.40 − £60.34
14 £40 − £5.60
15 £60 − £37.80
16 £408.04 − £89.30
17 £3.07 − 99p
18 £67.10 − £1.89
19 £80 − £6.74
20 £700 − £60.89

C Find an approximate answer **and** the exact result. Show the numbers used for the approximation.
1 £46.78 + £6.89
2 £321.56 + £67.89
3 £67.82 − £48.94
4 £7.89 + £26.87
5 £789.51 − £194.87
6 £67.89 + £67.47
7 £6.78 − £6.59
8 £74.68 − £7.47
9 £681.53 − £592.43
10 £78.24 − £8.37
11 £167.35 − £68.60
12 £6020.70 − £938.82
13 £400.10 − £67.20
14 £468.99 + £24.85
15 £46.90 + £301.78
16 £468.70 + £28.96
17 £43.60 − £5.78
18 £3002 − £290.39
19 £68.36 + £641.38
20 £68.92 + £582.08

D 1 Find the sum of £2.30 and £1.37.
2 Find the difference between £3.23 and £5.19.
3 How much is £5.49 short of £6?
4 By how much does £7 exceed £6.87?
5 Find the difference between £68 and £4.56.
6 Write in words £1.20.
7 Write in figures four hundred pounds five pence.
8 By how much is £0.20 greater than 5p?
9 Find the total of £6.89 and £4.23.
10 When I spend £7.84, how much change do I get out of £10?

EXAMPLE
£3.24 × 3 = £9.72   £6.48 ÷ 4 = £1.62

A
1 £4.32 × 4
2 £6.21 × 3
3 £23.41 × 5
4 £34.02 × 5
5 £3.03 × 4
6 £5.61 × 4
7 £6.32 × 3
8 £12.15 × 5
9 £6.35 × 4
10 £3.24 × 5
11 £13.23 × 6
12 £4.25 × 6
13 £53.20 × 2
14 £43.23 × 4
15 £345 × 4
16 £25.64 × 5
17 £312.45 × 4
18 £23.40 × 6
19 £6.21 × 5
20 £134.35 × 2

B
1 £4.80 ÷ 2
2 £3.36 ÷ 3
3 £1.80 ÷ 6
4 £4.50 ÷ 3
5 £24.16 ÷ 4
6 £15.50 ÷ 5
7 £30.18 ÷ 6
8 £928 ÷ 4
9 £5.40 ÷ 4
10 £200.15 ÷ 5
11 £4.86 ÷ 2
12 £39.60 ÷ 3
13 £30.25 ÷ 5
14 £18.72 ÷ 6
15 £31.08 ÷ 2
16 £101.72 ÷ 4
17 £20.10 ÷ 5
18 £46.08 ÷ 3
19 £96.24 ÷ 6
20 £130.65 ÷ 3

C Find an approximate value and exact answer. Show the numbers used for the approximation.
1 £4.69 × 7
2 £31.35 × 6
3 £7.24 × 8
4 £8.42 × 5
5 £67.41 × 9
6 £4.78 × 5
7 £6.90 × 6
8 £84.61 × 8
9 £73.25 × 4
10 £7.92 × 7
11 £6.45 × 8
12 £9.10 × 9
13 £67.19 × 5
14 £27.25 × 9
15 £6.93 × 7
16 £21.75 × 6
17 £237.50 × 8
18 £4.65 × 6
19 £4.08 × 5
20 £70.03 × 8

D Make an estimate for each answer and show the numbers used.
Calculate the exact value.

1 £19.32 ÷ 7
2 £4.86 ÷ 9
3 £288.60 ÷ 6
4 £1.36 ÷ 8
5 £40.40 ÷ 8

6 £98.70 ÷ 7
7 £235.20 ÷ 6
8 £91.76 ÷ 8
9 £51.54 ÷ 6
10 £381 ÷ 5

11 £210.60 ÷ 9
12 £207.24 ÷ 4
13 £2107.44 ÷ 9
14 £33.95 ÷ 5
15 £41.36 ÷ 8

$26p \times 100 = £26.00$ $£7.20 \div 10 = 72p$ $£2.05 \times 40 = £20.50 \times 4$
$£2.04 \times 100 = £204.00$ $£16 \div 100 = 16p$ $= £82$

A		B		C	
1	$4p \times 10$	1	$£4.68 \times 10$	1	$£4 \times 20$
2	$15p \times 10$	2	$£34.24 \times 10$	2	$£4.10 \times 20$
3	$7p \times 100$	3	$£46.70 \times 100$	3	$£3.02 \times 40$
4	$35p \times 10$	4	$£6.70 \times 100$	4	$£6.51 \times 200$
5	$59p \times 10$	5	$£34.50 \times 10$	5	$£14.03 \times 50$
6	$£3.20 \times 10$	6	$£32.20 \div 10$	6	$£1.03 \times 500$
7	$£5.16 \times 100$	7	$£67.80 \div 10$	7	$£3.04 \times 60$
8	$£4.01 \times 10$	8	$£43.20 \times 100$	8	$£1.23 \times 400$
9	$37p \times 100$	9	$£134.50 \div 10$	9	$£1.15 \times 400$
10	$£1.06 \times 100$	10	$£45 \div 100$	10	$£42.15 \times 30$
11	$£5.20 \div 10$	11	$£678 \div 10$	11	$£2.33 \times 50$
12	$£7 \div 100$	12	$£67 \times 10$	12	$£2.24 \times 500$
13	$£19.20 \div 10$	13	$£567 \times 10$	13	$£21.15 \times 40$
14	$£54.70 \div 10$	14	$£632 \div 100$	14	$£100.24 \times 300$
15	$£63 \div 100$	15	$£46.40 \div 10$	15	$£6.35 \times 20$
16	$60p \div 10$	16	$£4.36 \times 10$	16	$£1.05 \times 400$
17	$£8.60 \div 10$	17	$£4.30 \times 100$	17	$£12.03 \times 600$
18	$£150 \div 100$	18	$£7.89 \times 10$	18	$£5.04 \times 60$
19	$£35 \div 100$	19	$£400.10 \div 10$	19	$£13.04 \times 500$
20	$£74 \div 10$	20	$£64.30 \div 10$	20	$£1.26 \times 30$

D 1 Kate bought a 1.13 kg chicken priced 99p and a 900 g bag of peas priced 70p. How much change should she get from a £5 note?

2 Pete plans to save £4.50 each week from his Saturday job to buy a sweater which costs £20. How many weeks will it take him?

3 John is paid £105 weekly for 52 weeks and Ken is paid £450 a month. Who is better paid, and by how much?

4 What coins would be needed to make exactly 39p using as few coins as possible?

5 I have exactly 57p in my purse and just 5 coins. What are the coins?

EXAMPLE

£15.21 × 43 = £654.03
```
  1521
    43
 60840
  4563
 65403
```

£3.05 × 24 = £73.20
```
  305
   24
 6100
 1220
 7320
```

£3.60 ÷ 30 = 36p ÷ 3
             = 12p

A
1. £1.26 × 23
2. £2.40 × 31
3. £31.04 × 34
4. £5.21 × 42
5. £2.23 × 15
6. £14.23 × 35
7. £3.02 × 16
8. £24.25 × 35
9. £14.21 × 25
10. £6.03 × 44
11. £2.05 × 14
12. £6.23 × 31
13. £61 × 62
14. £46.32 × 51
15. £35.20 × 41
16. £4.56 × 33
17. £3.45 × 24
18. £4.32 × 15
19. £1.43 × 53
20. £15.36 × 32

B
1. £1.20 ÷ 20
2. £8 ÷ 200
3. £7.20 ÷ 30
4. £520 ÷ 400
5. £103 ÷ 50
6. £9 ÷ 60
7. £612 ÷ 300
8. £2020 ÷ 40
9. £122 ÷ 20
10. £6200 ÷ 500
11. £137.20 ÷ 70
12. £3360 ÷ 800
13. £260 ÷ 50
14. £15.60 ÷ 60
15. £6840 ÷ 900
16. £485.40 ÷ 60
17. £170 ÷ 500
18. £1211 ÷ 70
19. £363 ÷ 40
20. £425 ÷ 500

C Estimate the answer and show the numbers used for it. Use a calculator to find the exact value.
1. 35p × 71
2. 86p × 28
3. £1.95 × 37
4. £6.03 × 19
5. £5.75 × 84
6. £67.80 × 56
7. £18.05 × 62
8. £58.92 × 81
9. £5.19 × 73
10. £6.37 × 59
11. 38p × 64
12. £4.57 × 17
13. £35.18 × 83
14. £1.65 × 58
15. £6.16 × 26
16. £81.49 × 39
17. £7.18 × 18
18. £72.07 × 57
19. £8.91 × 87
20. £65.25 × 96

D Give the answers correct to the nearest £1. Do not use a calculator.
1. £62.60 ÷ 12
2. £57.80 ÷ 10
3. £67.25 ÷ 11
4. £105.34 ÷ 5
5. £320.45 ÷ 8
6. £69.50 ÷ 12
7. £89.65 ÷ 8
8. £36.05 ÷ 6
9. £302.15 ÷ 10
10. £639.08 ÷ 8
11. £43.56 ÷ 8
12. £21.45 ÷ 5
13. £68.36 ÷ 6
14. £70.68 ÷ 8
15. £567.35 ÷ 7

WAGES AND EXPENSES

September

S	M	T	W	T	F	S
				1	2	3
4	5	6	7	8	9	10
11	12	13	14	15	16	17
18	19	20	21	22	23	24
25	26	27	28	29	30	

Use this calendar to answer questions 1 to 5.

1 The pupils from a certain school have to go to other centres and can reclaim their fares. Term started on 6th September. Find how much these pupils can claim for their fares in September:

John goes every Friday and his return fare is 80p.

Mary goes every Monday and her return fare is 40p.

Ken goes on Mondays and Thursdays. Both days the return fare is 60p.

Tom is absent from 19th to 21st. He goes on Tuesdays. The return fare is 40p.

2 Linda is at work every Saturday from 8.30 am to 4.30 pm. How many hours is this?

She is allowed a total of 1 hour for lunch and coffee breaks, but is not paid for this time. How many hours is she paid for?

Her wage is £1.50 an hour. How much is she paid each Saturday?

She says her tips for September averaged £4 a day. How much did she receive altogether including tips during September?

3 Ken earns £1.25 a day, but cannot work on Sundays. If he works every day he can, how much will he earn in September?

4 Mary starts work on 18th September and works for two hours on every day to the end of the month. She is normally paid £1.20 an hour, but she gets time and a half for Sundays. How much does she earn in September?

5 Bill is normally paid an hourly rate of £2.40. His overtime rate is time and a quarter. How much is his overtime rate?

From 12th to 16th September he was able to work 2 hours overtime each day. How much was he paid for overtime in that week?

6 Arthur's basic pay is £90 a week and overtime is paid at £4 an hour. In a week when he does 10 hours overtime, how much is his total pay?

How much overtime must he do to earn £150 in a week?

7 Bill earns £144 for a 36 hour week. What rate of pay is this? Bill is paid time and a quarter for overtime. What is his overtime rate?

In a week when he works 40 hours, how much will he be paid?

8 Mr Jones employs 10 people. The 3 juniors are paid £65 a week each and the others are paid £110 each. What is his total wages bill for a week?

9 Mrs Brown pays two people £50 a week, and three others £66 a week. How much does she pay these 5 people?

10 Three jobs are advertised. One rate of pay is £85 per week, another is £350 per month and the third is £4100 per annum. Which is the highest rate of pay?

FOREIGN CURRENCY

A Copy and complete this table. A calculator is unnecessary.

UK £	Belgium francs	Greece drachmas
£1	15.4	245
£2	30.8	490
£3		
£5		
£10		
£15		
£25		
£50		
£100		

Use your table to find the value of:

1. £8 in francs
2. £20 in drachmas
3. £30 in francs
4. £40 in francs
5. £56 in drachmas
6. £75 in drachmas
7. £110 in francs
8. £65 in drachmas
9. £150 in drachmas
10. £250 in francs
11. 500 drachmas to the nearest £
12. 12 500 drachmas to the nearest £
13. 1050 francs to the nearest £
14. 3275 francs to the nearest £
15. 6670 francs to the nearest £

B 1 When I was on holiday the rate of exchange was 204 pesetas for £1. About how many pesetas should I expect when I change £10 worth of travellers cheques?

My friend changed £15. About how many pesetas was this?

2 When Mr Jones took his family to Greece the exchange was 241 drachmas to the £1. About how much would he get for £50?

Mrs Jones wanted a blouse that was priced 2500 drachmas. Would that have been more or less than £12?

A bus fare was 95 drachmas per person. If children had to pay full fare and Mr Jones wanted to pay for his wife and two children, should he offer 500 or 400 drachmas? How much change should he expect?

His daughter paid 700 drachmas for a sun hat. Was that more or less than £3?

3 Mr Dixon went to Japan on business at a time when the rate of exchange was about 230 yen to the pound. The hotel account was for 23 000 yen. How much was that?

He was offered a piece of equipment which cost 4500 yen. Was that more or less than £20, £200?

4 Mr Smith went to Germany and found the exchange rate was 3.15 marks to the pound. He wanted to buy a jacket priced at 320 marks and a shirt which cost 75 marks. Were these more or less than £10, £15, £20, £25, £30, £50, £100?

5 When the exchange rate in the Netherlands was 3.46 guilders to the £1, about how many guilders could be expected for £50, £100?

A box of chocolates was priced 35 guilders. About how much was this?

31

7 ratio, proportion and speed

EXAMPLE

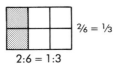

²⁄₆ = ⅓

2:6 = 1:3

4:6 = 2:3

6 divided in the ratio 2 : 1 gives 4 in 1 part, 2 in the other part.

A Simplify:
1 3 : 6
2 5 : 10
3 3 : 9
4 4 : 8
5 3 : 12
6 24 : 8
7 4 : 12
8 4 : 16
9 4 : 20
10 2 lb : 4 lb
11 5 oz : 10 oz
12 3 cm : 6 cm
13 4 cm : 6 cm
14 2 ft : 4 ft
15 3 yd : 6 yd
16 4 m : 6 m
17 3 oz : 6 oz
18 2 miles : 4 miles
19 6 cm : 4 cm
20 6 cm : 3 cm

B Simplify:
1 5 : 15
2 7 : 21
3 8 : 24
4 9 : 27
5 6 : 30
6 7 : 28
7 6 : 42
8 8 : 56
9 9 : 54
10 8 : 72
11 12 : 18
12 14 : 16
13 20 : 24
14 30 : 32
15 36 : 48
16 35 : 42
17 27 : 26
18 45 : 54
19 27 : 48
20 36 : 60

C Divide:
1 6 in the ratio 2 : 1
2 12 in the ratio 1 : 3
3 20 in the ratio 2 : 3
4 24 in the ratio 3 : 1
5 15 in the ratio 2 : 3
6 £6 in the ratio 1 : 2
7 £9 in the ratio 2 : 1
8 £12 in the ratio 2 : 3
9 £10 in the ratio 4 : 1
10 £25 in the ratio 3 : 2
11 9 m in the ratio 2 : 1
12 18 yd in the ratio 5 : 1
13 20 cm in the ratio 3 : 2
14 10 cm in the ratio 1 : 3
15 100 m in the ratio 3 : 7
16 50 lb in the ratio 1 : 4
17 300 g in the ratio 5 : 1
18 7 lb in the ratio 3 : 4
19 90 kg in the ratio 4 : 5
20 500 kg in the ratio 3 : 2

D Measure the lines in questions 1–10 in centimetres and the lines in questions 11–18 in inches. Find the ratio of the lengths of each pair.

1 ─────────   ──────

2 ──────────────

3 ───────────────────

4 ──────────────────────

5 ──────   ──────

6 ──────────────────

7 ───

8 ─────────   ───────

9 ──────────────

10 ──────────────

11 ──────   ────

12 ──────────

13 ────────────────

14 ──────────────────

15 ──────────   ────

16 ──────────────────

17 ──────────   ──────

18 ──────────────────────

32

TRAVELLING BY ROAD

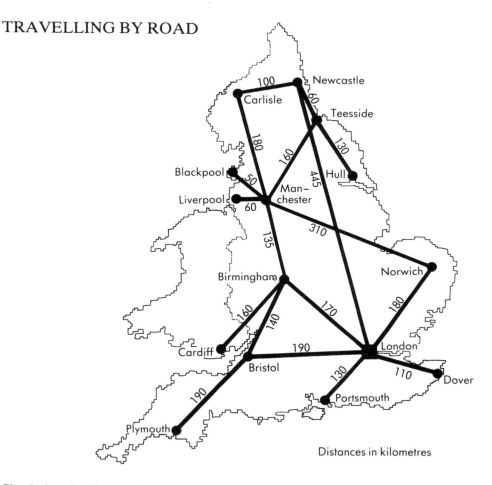

Distances in kilometres

A Check that the distance from Birmingham to Carlisle is shown as 315 km.
Use the map to find these distances:

1 London to Newcastle

2 London to Plymouth via Bristol

3 Cardiff to Liverpool via Birmingham and Manchester

4 Liverpool to Teesside

5 Portsmouth to Norwich

6 Norwich to Dover via London

7 Birmingham to Plymouth

8 Norwich to Blackpool via Manchester

9 Plymouth to Norwich via Bristol and London

10 Birmingham to Dover

B 1 A coach journey from London to Plymouth is scheduled to take 4½ hours. It leaves London at 0900 hours. When is it expected to arrive in Plymouth?

2 A bus company advertisement in Birmingham says 'Travel by bus and be in Plymouth by 5.00 pm'.
The bus leaves at 11.30 am. How long does the journey take?
There is a 30 minute break at Bristol. What is the average speed of the bus?

3 A bus left Norwich at 9.25 am and arrived in London at 12.45 pm.
How long did the journey take?
What was the average speed for this journey if there was a 20 minute coffee stop?

33

EXAMPLE

If a boy walks at 6 kilometres per hour, he will take 2 hours to walk 12 kilometres.

$12 \div 6 = 2$ hours

```
0        6        12
└┴┴┴┴┴┴┴┴┴┴┴┴┴┴┴┴┘
```

If a boy walks at 5 kilometres per hour, he will take 3 hours to walk 15 kilometres.

$$\frac{15}{5} = 3 \text{ hours}$$

```
0        5      10      15
└┴┴┴┴┴┴┴┴┴┴┴┴┴┴┴┴┴┴┴┘
```

A Find the time taken to travel:

1 20 km at 4 km/h
2 10 km at 5 km/h
3 16 km at 4 km/h
4 14 km at 2 km/h
5 18 km at 2 km/h
6 25 miles at 5 miles/h
7 30 km at 5 km/h
8 27 km at 3 km/h
9 21 km at 3 km/h
10 22 km at 2 km/h
11 45 km at 5 km/h
12 35 km at 5 km/h
13 32 miles at 4 miles/h
14 15 km at 3 km/h
15 28 km at 4 km/h
16 36 km at 3 km/h
17 36 km at 4 km/h
18 24 miles at 3 miles/h
19 55 km at 5 km/h
20 40 km at 4 km/h

B How long are these journeys expected to take? The speed is the expected average. Give the time correct to the nearest ½ hour.

1 360 miles at 60 mph
2 510 miles at 50 mph
3 4600 miles at 450 mph
4 3000 miles at 450 mph
5 205 miles at 50 mph
6 160 km at 80 km/h
7 156 km at 80 km/h
8 245 km at 60 km/h
9 75 km at 70 km/h
10 2105 km at 700 km/h
11 1900 km at 600 km/h
12 50 km at 25 km/h
13 41 km at 20 km/h
14 57 km at 15 km/h
15 35 km at 12 km/h

What kind of transport was used for these journeys?

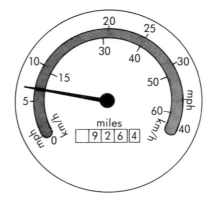

C Terry has an odometer on his bicycle. It shows speeds in both mph and km/h.

1 What speed in mph is it showing now? What is this in km/h?
2 It also shows the total distance travelled in miles. The last digit is tenths of a mile. What distance is it showing?
3 How much further has he to travel until it shows one thousand miles?
4 Terry uses his bike to do a paper round each day. On Monday before setting out he noted that the mileage reading was 902.8 miles. During the week he used his bike for the paper round only. When he finished on Friday the reading was 922.8 miles. How many miles had he cycled? What was the daily mileage for his round?

34

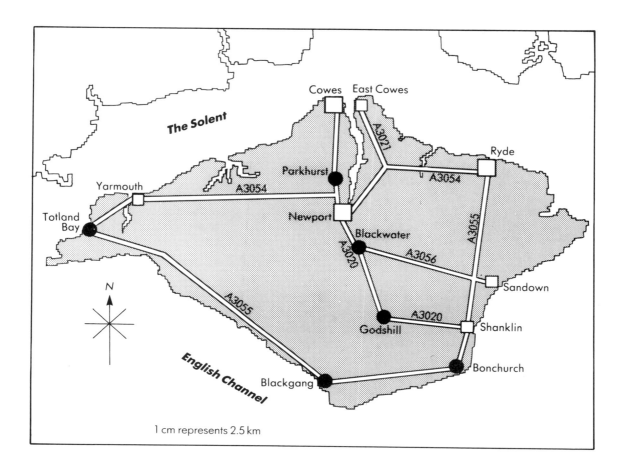

1 cm represents 2.5 km

THE ISLE OF WIGHT

1 Start at Totland Bay. Follow the road A3055. Where does it end?
2 What is the other road number from Ryde back to Totland Bay?
3 From Blackgang go east along A _____ to Bonchurch.
4 From Ryde go _____ along A _____ to Sandown.
5 From Yarmouth go _____ along A _____ to Parkhurst.
6 From Totland Bay go south-east along A _____ to Blackgang.
7 From Newport go _____ along _____ to Cowes.
8 Go east from Godshill to _____. Then go south to _____.
9 Go south-west from Yarmouth to _____. Then go _____ to Blackgang.
10 Go west from Ryde then south-west to Newport. Then go _____
   along _____ to Blackwater.
11 Go _____ from East Cowes to A3054. Then go east to _____.
12 Go _____ from Parkhurst to Blackwater. Then go _____ to Sandown.
13 Which roads do you use from Yarmouth to Newport?
14 Which roads do you use from Bonchurch to Godshill?
15 Which roads do you use from Cowes to Blackwater and Sandown?
16 How far is Totland Bay from Blackgang?
17 How far is Shanklin from Ryde?
18 A man living in Shanklin has to travel daily to Ryde. It is a busy road
   and he finds it usually takes 15 minutes each way. What is his average speed?

JAM AND MARMALADE

A I will use 2 lemons for the lemon curd.
How many eggs will I need?
How much sugar will I need?
How much butter will I need?

Lemon Curd
1 lemon
100 g sugar
1 egg
50 g butter

B 1 I have 3 kg strawberries for jam making.
How many lemons will I need?
How much sugar will I have to use?

2 I have 1½ kg strawberries for jam.
How many lemons will I use?
How much sugar will I have to use?

Strawberry Jam

1 kg strawberries
1 lemon
1 kg sugar

MARY WATSON'S BLACKCU... JAM 1987

C 1 I have 2 kg of gooseberries.
How much sugar do I need?

2 Ann has 3 kg of gooseberries.
How much sugar will she need?

3 Mary has picked 4 kg of gooseberries.
How much sugar will she need?

Gooseberry Jam
1 kg gooseberries
1 kg 225g sugar

D 1 I have picked 2 kg of blackcurrants.
How much sugar will I need?

2 Jane has 3 kg blackcurrants.
How much sugar will she need?

JAMS

Blackcurrant Jam

1kg blackcurrants
1½ kg sugar

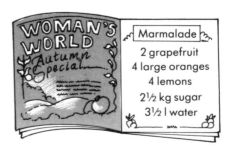

E 1 I have 4 grapefruits and 8 lemons for
marmalade.
How many oranges should I use?
How much sugar do I need?
How much water should I use?

2 Try to work out how much it costs to
make this marmalade. It would fill
about 9 jars.
Is it cheaper to make your own
marmalade?

WOMAN'S WORLD Autumn Special

Marmalade
2 grapefruit
4 large oranges
4 lemons
2½ kg sugar
3½ l water

ROASTING CHART

These are the times needed to roast meat.

Beef	40 minutes per kg + 20 minutes
Leg of lamb	40 minutes per kg + 20 minutes
Leg of pork	50 minutes per kg + 25 minutes
Gammon	40 minutes per kg + 20 minutes
Turkey	40 minutes per kg + 20 minutes
Chicken	40 minutes per kg
Goose	40 minutes per kg
Pheasant	1 hour 30 minutes
Grouse	1 hour

A How long would it take to cook:

1. 2 kg of beef?
2. a 3 kg chicken?
3. a 6 kg turkey?
4. a 5 kg goose?
5. a grouse?
6. a pheasant?
7. 1 kg of gammon?
8. a 2 kg leg of pork?
9. a 2 kg leg of lamb?
10. a 3 kg leg of lamb?

B When would these pieces of meat be cooked:

1. A 2 kg chicken put in the oven at 11 am?
2. A 5 kg turkey put in the oven at 8.30 am?
3. A pheasant put in at 11.30 am?
4. 1 kg of gammon put in the oven at 6.30 pm?
5. A goose (4 kg) put in at 9 am?

C These should be cooked by 12.45 pm.
When should they be put into the oven?

1. A 1 kg chicken.
2. 2 kg of gammon.
3. A pheasant.
4. A 1½ kg leg of pork.
5. A 4 kg turkey.

There is a 24 hour digital timer on the cooker. If it is set for the starting time, the oven will switch on automatically. What time should be set for these?

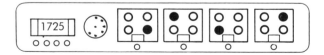

BARGAINS

A 1 How much do you pay for 2 bars of Toffee-Choc?
  2 How much will 1 bar weigh?
  3 Is there a cheaper way of getting the same weight?

B 1 What is the cheapest way of buying 4 oz of Creamy Special?
  2 If you buy two 3 oz bars how much will it cost?
  3 How much cheaper is it than six 1 oz bars?

C 1 If you have 70p to spend, which packs would you choose to get most crisps?
  2 How much would each pack weigh in the Bumper Size?
  3 Which is the cheapest way to buy a lot of crisps?

D 1 Which is the cheapest way to buy 6 pairs of tights?
  2 How much does it save?

E 1 If you buy one 40 g and two 20 g bars, how much do they weigh and cost?
  2 What is the cheapest way of buying 120 g Crispy Crunch?

F If you want a lot of biscuits, which is the cheapest way to buy them?

A A group of people went to a town 10 km away.

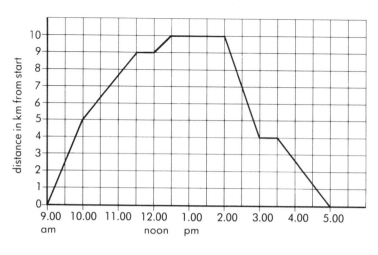

1 How long did it take them to travel the first kilometre? How do you think they were travelling?

2 When did they have their first stop?

3 What was their average speed between 9.00 and 11.30 am?

4 How long did they stop at lunchtime?

5 When did they start the return journey?

6 How long did they rest on the return journey?

7 How fast were they walking between 3.30 and 5.0 pm?

8 What was their fastest walking speed?

9 What was the total distance they walked?

10 How many hours were they actually walking?

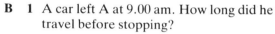

B 1 A car left A at 9.00 am. How long did he travel before stopping?

2 How fast did he travel before stopping?

3 How fast did he travel on the second part of his journey?

4 Another car left a town 70 km from A. How long did he travel before stopping?

5 How fast did he travel at first?

6 How long did he stop?

7 When did the first car pass him?

8 How far were the cars from A when they passed?

9 What was the fastest speed travelled? Which car travelled fastest?

10 What was the second car's average speed for the whole journey?

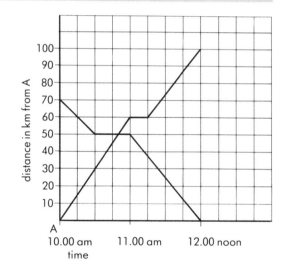

8 weight

HOW HEAVY?

A Look at this ½ lb tub of margarine. It says it weighs . . . g.

Think about the weights of these. Put them in order, heaviest first.

227g

Jam
454g

Sugar
908g

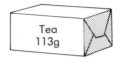
Tea
113g

Toffees
227g

B These are the weight labels for the items below. Think where they belong.

Copy and complete this list:

1 lb rice weighs _____

½ lb butter _____

packet of biscuits _____

small tin of baby food _____

200g

biscuits

454g

butter

100g

rice

227g

tin of baby food

C Kilograms are used for weighing heavy things. (1 kilogram is about 2.2 lb)

Put these weights where you think is sensible: 65 kg, 30 kg, 6 kg.

1

2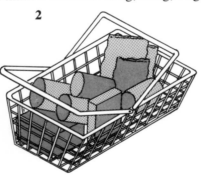

3

D Kilograms are often called kilos. Think which weight label should go on each packet:

1 kilo, 2 kilo, ½ kilo. Make a list.

Bag of potatoes _____

9 eating apples _____

2 bananas _____

EXAMPLE

	kg	hg	Dg	g
1000 g = 1 kilogram	7	0	2	0

7.02 kg = 7020 g

A Express in kilograms:

1 100 g
2 350 g
3 5000 g
4 6500 g
5 70 g
6 450 g
7 4500 g
8 3020 g
9 15 000 g
10 850 g
11 60 500 g
12 3750 g
13 680 g
14 3400 g
15 23 000 g
16 890 g
17 868 g
18 8680 g
19 60 700 g
20 20 960 g

B Express in grams:

1 1 kg
2 1.5 kg
3 0.5 kg
4 3.5 kg
5 70 kg
6 0.02 kg
7 6.08 kg
8 15.9 kg
9 0.07 kg
10 0.6 kg
11 0.04 kg
12 0.042 kg
13 7.03 kg
14 0.905 kg
15 0.0032 kg
16 0.0026 kg
17 4.008 kg
18 0.01 kg
19 0.0021 kg
20 8.3 kg

C Express to the nearest kilogram:

1 5.78 kg
2 11.9 kg
3 23.6 kg
4 81.3 kg
5 756.9 kg
6 950 g
7 1800 g
8 5600 g
9 1209 g
10 7456 g
11 560 g + 600 g
12 800 g + 2 kg
13 700 g + 900 g
14 2.6 kg + 11.5 kg
15 360 g × 100
16 450 g × 200
17 54 g × 600
18 37 g × 800
19 60 g × 500
20 30 g × 480

D The graph converts pounds to kilograms.

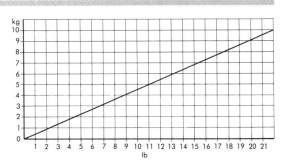

1 What is the metric equivalent of 9 lb?
2 A box weighs 4 lb. What would it weigh on metric scales?
3 A bag of sugar weighs 1 kg. What is this in lb?
4 A case weighs 8 kg. How many pounds is this?
5 A crate weighs 50 kg. How many pounds is this?
6 A boy weighs 120 lb. How many kg does he weigh?
7 A girl weighs 60 kg. How many pounds is this?
8 A child weighs 70 lb. How many kg is this?

41

9 length

EXAMPLE

km	hm	Dm	m	dm	cm	mm	
							1000 m = 1 km 100 cm = 1 m
5	0	0	0				5 km = 5000 m
		2	3				23 m = 0.023 km
			4	0	0	0	4 m = 400 cm = 4000 mm
					3	1	3.1 cm = 31 mm = 0.031 m

A Express in km:

1 55 m
2 176 m
3 47 m
4 126 m
5 315 m
6 56 m
7 23 m
8 47 m
9 357 m
10 2345 m
11 6002 m
12 7300 m
13 4500 m
14 670 m
15 8005 m
16 7000 m
17 3090 m
18 5000 m
19 30 m
20 500 m

B Express in metres:

1 4.5 km
2 6.8 km
3 0.8 km
4 0.75 km
5 0.4 km
6 5.4 km
7 0.66 km
8 1.66 km
9 0.9 km
10 4.6 km
11 0.09 km
12 0.009 km
13 0.02 km
14 6.07 km
15 2.006 km
16 0.0007 km
17 0.004 km
18 5.07 km
19 12.5 km
20 0.001 km

C Express in cm:

1 2 m
2 5 m
3 4.5 m
4 0.5 m
5 6.05 m
6 0.05 m
7 0.04 m
8 0.004 m
9 3.75 m
10 12.3 m
11 56 mm
12 67 mm
13 85 mm
14 126 mm
15 378 mm
16 7 mm
17 146 mm
18 9 mm
19 34 mm
20 200 mm

D
1 Express 40 cm in mm.
2 Which is longer, 50 mm or 0.1 m?
3 Which is shorter, 199 m or 0.02 km?
4 By how much is 0.05 km longer than 20 m?
5 By how much is 67 mm shorter than 10 cm?
6 Express 23.1 cm in mm.
7 A line measures 6.3 cm. What is this in mm?
8 By how much is 76 cm short of 1 metre?
9 By how much does 456 m exceed 0.0456 km?
10 What is the difference between 0.05 m and 0.005 m?

EXAMPLE

$235\,cm \times 20 = 4700\,cm$
$= 47\,m$

$100\,cm = 1\,metre$
$1000\ \ m = 1\,kilometre$

A Give the answer in metres.

1 14.6 cm + 5.4 cm
2 34.5 cm + 6.5 cm
3 56.7 cm + 15.4 cm
4 2.3 cm + 15.6 cm
5 67 cm + 33.5 cm
6 15.6 cm − 8.6 cm
7 27 cm − 9.8 cm
8 4.7 cm − 3.9 cm
9 67.1 cm − 7.8 cm
10 23.5 cm − 18.7 cm

11 45 m + 36.4 m
12 34.6 m + 25 m
13 56.7 m + 3 m
14 5.6 m + 8.9 m
15 17.4 m + 5.9 m
16 126 km − 89 km
17 35 km − 32.5 km
18 450 km − 390 km
19 34 km − 25.6 km
20 756 km − 749 km

B Give the answer in metres.

1 23.5 cm × 10
2 36.5 cm × 30
3 45.6 cm × 400
4 6.5 cm × 300
5 25 cm × 800
6 580 cm ÷ 10
7 840 cm ÷ 20
8 360 cm ÷ 3
9 420 cm ÷ 20
10 780 cm ÷ 30

11 34.5 m × 7
12 3.5 m × 20
13 54.2 m × 5
14 23.5 m × 8
15 12.6 m × 50
16 400 km ÷ 5
17 320 km ÷ 80
18 5600 km ÷ 700
19 480 km ÷ 30
20 960 km ÷ 40

C **1** A ball of string was cut into 20 cm lengths. The pieces were put into bundles of 10 and 7 bundles were made. How much string was there in the ball?

Altogether 350 pieces of string will be needed. How many more balls of the same size as the first will be needed?

2 The circumference of a wheel is 70 cm. How far has it travelled when it is rolled along the ground and turns 100 times?

3 When a car wheel turns once it rolls 180 cm. How far would 50 turns take it?

A van wheel travels 215 cm when it rolls once. How much further than the car wheel would 50 turns take it?
How many times does a car wheel turn when it travels 1 kilometre?
How many times does the van wheel turn when it travels 1 kilometre?

4 I need 3.2 m of fabric for each curtain length and 6 of these lengths. I have chosen a fabric which costs £7.50 a metre. For the lining I need six 3 m lengths and that costs £2 per metre.
The tape and hooks will cost £12.

What will be the total cost for making these curtains?

5 Fencing wire costs 70p a metre. If there is no wastage, how much will it cost to enclose a square of side 4.1 m?

EXAMPLE

The perimeter of this rectangle is $2(5 + 2) = 14$ cm

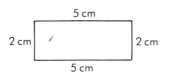

The perimeter of this shape is $5 + 5 + 5 + 5 + 5 + 5 = 30$ cm

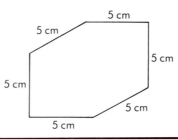

The circumference of a circle is πd. $\pi = 3.14$

Circumference $= 3.14 \times 10$ cm $= 31.4$ cm

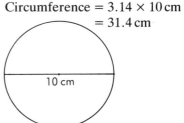

A Find the perimeter of these rectangles:

	length	breadth		length	breadth		length	breadth
1	3 cm	5 cm	**6**	3 yd	4 yd	**11**	15 cm	12 cm
2	4 in	1 in	**7**	6 cm	3 cm	**12**	23 cm	15 cm
3	6 cm	4 cm	**8**	5 yd	6 yd	**13**	14 cm	24 cm
4	7 cm	3 cm	**9**	6 cm	6 cm	**14**	24 yd	22 yd
5	5 cm	4 cm	**10**	2 cm	6 cm	**15**	31 cm	24 cm

B Find the circumference of these circles (use $\pi = 3.14$):

1	diameter = 5 cm	**6**	diameter = 30 cm	**11**	diameter = 4.5 cm
2	diameter = 6 cm	**7**	diameter = 40 cm	**12**	diameter = 6.3 cm
3	diameter = 20 cm	**8**	diameter = 50 cm	**13**	diameter = 8.9 cm
4	diameter = 6 cm	**9**	diameter = 9 cm	**14**	diameter = 7.2 cm
5	diameter = 8 cm	**10**	diameter = 2 cm	**15**	diameter = 5.5 cm

C Find the perimeter of these shapes:

1
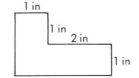

2
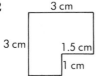

3
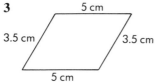

4
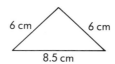

5
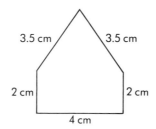

6
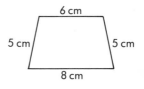

7

8
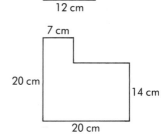

44

Perimeter is the distance all round the shape.

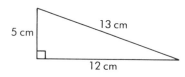

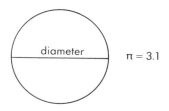

Perimeter = 5 + 7 + 5 +
       7 cm= 24 cm

Perimeter = 5 + 12 + 13 cm
       = 30 cm

Circumference = πd
e.g. radius = 5 cm
Circumference = 3.1 × 10 cm
             = 31 cm

A Calculate the perimeter of these rectangles:

	length	breadth
1	2 cm	3 cm
2	4 cm	5 cm
3	5 cm	2 cm
4	5 cm	6.5 cm
5	6 cm	10 cm
6	7 cm	4.5 cm
7	6 cm	7.6 cm
8	9 cm	5.7 cm
9	8 cm	7.5 cm
10	7 m	5.4 m
11	12 m	15 m
12	20 m	35 m
13	25 m	56 m
14	30 m	45 m
15	40 m	12 m

B Calculate the perimeter of triangles with these sides:

1 3 cm, 4 cm, 6 cm
2 12 cm, 8 cm, 7 cm
3 4 cm, 7 cm, 5 cm
4 6 cm, 6 cm, 6 cm
5 4 cm, 6 cm, 7 cm
6 4 cm, 6.5 cm, 7 cm
7 3 cm, 3.5 cm, 3.5 cm
8 15 cm, 15 cm, 12 cm
9 8 cm, 7.5 cm, 7.5 cm
10 9 cm, 9 cm, 9 cm
11 14 cm, 8 cm, 8 cm
12 6 cm, 5.6 cm, 5.6 cm
13 4 cm, 4.6 cm, 4.6 cm
14 4.5 cm, 4.6 cm, 4.7 cm
15 6.2 cm, 6.2 cm, 6.2 cm

C Calculate the circumference of these circles. Use $\pi = 3.1$.

1 diameter = 5 cm
2 diameter = 4 cm
3 diameter = 7 cm
4 diameter = 10 cm
5 diameter = 9 cm
6 diameter = 20 cm
7 diameter = 3 cm
8 diameter = 4.5 cm
9 diameter = 6.6 cm
10 diameter = 1 cm
11 radius = 7.5 cm
12 radius = 3.5 cm
13 radius = 6.5 cm
14 radius = 5.7 cm
15 radius = 7.9 cm

D Find the perimeter of these shapes. They are drawn on a 1 cm grid.

1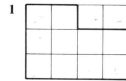

2

3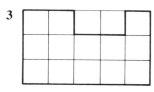

E A man has 28 panels of fencing. Each panel is 2 m long and 1 m high. Draw sketches to show the measurements of the rectangles he could enclose with these panels. NB. A panel must not be split.

F A farmer wishes to make an enclosure against a long wall. Part of the wall is to be used as one side. He has 20 m of wire for the other 3 sides. If he uses all the wire, make sketches of some of the rectangular enclosures he could make.

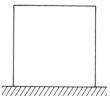

HEIGHT AND ARMSPAN

John is 157 cm tall.
His armspan is 158 cm.

A 1 How tall is Ray?
   2 How tall is Tim?
   3 How tall is Sally?
   4 How tall is Mary?
   5 How tall is Bill?
   6 How tall is Ann?

Height

160 cm — Ray, John
155 cm — Janet, Andrew
150 cm — Tim, Sandra, Carol
145 cm — Tony, Judith
              Sally
140 cm — Mary, Joan
135 cm — Ann, Bill
130 cm —

130 cm   140 cm   150 cm   160 cm

ARMSPAN

B 1 What is Bill's armspan?
   2 What is Tony's armspan?
   3 What is Carol's armspan?
   4 What is Judith's armspan?
   5 What is Joan's armspan?
   6 What is Andrew's armspan?

C 1 How many pupils are more than 150 cm tall?
   2 How many pupils are just 150 cm tall?
   3 How many pupils are less than 140 cm tall?
   4 How many pupils are just 140 cm tall?
   5 Who is the tallest pupil?
   6 Who is the shortest girl?

D 1 Which pupils have an armspan the same as their height?
   2 Which pupils have an armspan less than their height?

E 1 Make a scattergraph for the height and armspan of the pupils in your class.
     Do the tall people have the longer arm spans?
   2 Make a scattergraph for the height and weight of your class.
     Are the tall people the heaviest?

46

SENDING A PARCEL

Parcels are weighed to find the cost of posting them. Most parcels are
standard size, but some are large size.

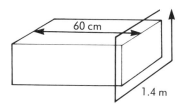

Standard size:
Up to 1.05 m long and 2 m combined length and girth.
e.g. This parcel is 60 cm long so it can be up to 1.4 m all round.

Large size:
Up to 1.5 m long and 3 m combined length and girth.

A Which of these things are standard size: an umbrella, a window pole, a
metre rule, 5 m dress material, a garden fork?

B These are the biggest size allowed. Find the missing measurement.

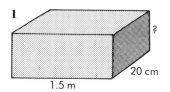

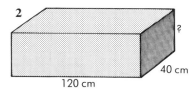

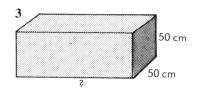

C How much string would you need to tie each of these parcels?
Allow an extra 10 cm on each parcel for knots.
Say whether these parcels are standard or large size.

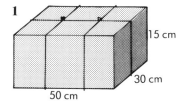

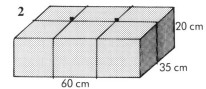

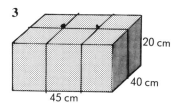

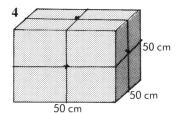

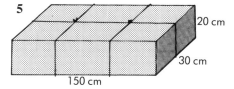

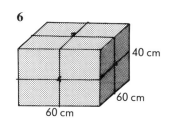

10 time

The clock shows 3.27
This is 27 minutes past 3.

Write the times shown by these clocks in two ways:

1

2

3

4

5

6

7

8

9

10

11

12

13

14

15

16

17

18

19

20

EXAMPLE

2.15

2.15 is quarter past 2

10.45

10.45 is quarter to 11

3.35

3.35 is 25 to 4

A Write these in words:
1 6.10
2 8.25
3 8.35
4 4.20
5 4.30
6 4.40
7 8.35
8 1.55
9 7.40
10 6.35
11 5.35
12 7.15
13 8.05
14 7.10
15 6.40
16 8.55
17 9.40
18 9.45
19 4.20
20 3.55

B Write these using minutes past the hour:
1 twenty-five to 2
2 quarter to 5
3 half past 6
4 five to 7
5 twenty-five to 8
6 quarter to 9
7 twenty to 1
8 ten to 8
9 quarter past 11
10 five to 12
11 twenty to 5
12 twenty past 3
13 quarter to 2
14 twenty-five past 6
15 ten to 4
16 twenty past 7
17 quarter to 11
18 twenty-five to 4
19 ten past 8
20 five to 10

C Write in words the time ten minutes after these:
1 10.15
2 9.30
3 3.20
4 5.40
5 6.05
6 7.20
7 10.40
8 8.05
9 11.50
10 6.55
11 7.30
12 2.50
13 6.05
14 4.15
15 9.20
16 1.35
17 6.50
18 11.05
19 5.55
20 9.25

D Write these using half or quarter:
1 3.15
2 4.30
3 8.15
4 10.15
5 4.45
6 10.30
7 8.45
8 6.15
9 1.45
10 7.45

Write these using minutes:
11 half past 6
12 quarter past 9
13 quarter to 11
14 quarter to 8
15 half past 4
16 quarter to 3
17 quarter past 10
18 quarter to 2
19 quarter past 7
20 quarter to 5

EXAMPLE

20 minutes past 10.
If it is before noon, then it is 10.20 am.
If it is after midday, then it is 10.20 pm or 22.20.

A Write these times using am or pm:

1 13.00
2 13.20
3 15.00
4 15.30
5 2.30
6 17.50
7 4.45
8 16.30
9 20.15
10 12.20
11 23.10
12 2.35
13 14.50
14 23.55
15 8.25
16 19.45
17 6.10
18 20.20
19 16.35
20 14.50

B Write these using the 24-hour clock:

1 9.10 am
2 2.30 pm
3 5.15 pm
4 6.12 pm
5 5.39 am
6 4.10 am
7 11.35 pm
8 9.04 pm
9 2.36 pm
10 5.09 am
11 4.56 pm
12 7.34 pm
13 8.30 pm
14 7.10 am
15 8.54 am
16 11.30 am
17 7.25 pm
18 5.02 am
19 8.50 pm
20 noon

C Write these in words using am or pm:

1 23.00
2 5.10
3 14.15
4 10.20
5 16.00
6 13.20
7 20.10
8 17.30
9 15.15
10 7.30
11 9.55
12 16.40
13 10.50
14 20.25
15 7.50
16 13.30
17 4.45
18 6.55
19 17.20
20 12.00

D Write in words the time half an hour before these times (use am, pm):

1 4.30
2 6.10
3 15.40
4 16.50
5 23.45
6 10.15
7 15.36
8 23.40
9 7.20
10 8.35
11 20.25
12 19.40
13 18.20
14 23.50
15 20.25
16 6.15
17 14.20
18 12.20
19 20.15
20 6.55

E Write the time

1 $1\frac{1}{2}$ hours before 10 pm
2 $\frac{3}{4}$ hour after 9.15 am
3 $2\frac{1}{4}$ hours before 1.00 pm
4 $\frac{1}{4}$ hour after 10.55 am
5 $\frac{1}{2}$ hour before 7.05 pm

6 15 minutes after 6.50 pm
7 10 minutes after 10.50 am
8 25 minutes before 11.10 am
9 35 minutes before 8.00 pm
10 45 minutes before 1.10 pm

50

FAMILY CARE

A Jim must take his dose of medicine every 4 hours.
He has the first dose at 9 am.
He takes 4 doses.
When must he take the others?

B Pat takes her pills every 4 hours.
She has the first at 8.30 am.
If she takes 3 further lots, when must she take them?

C Dick must take a dose 3 times a day.
He takes the first at 8 am and the last at 8 pm.
When should he take the others?

D Andrew must have a pill 3 times a day.
He has the first at 9 am. He is put to bed at 7 pm.
When should he be given the other ones?

E Grandma rests for $2\frac{1}{2}$ hours each afternoon.
When does she get up if

   1 On Monday she goes to bed at 2.30 pm?
   2 On Tuesday she goes to bed at 3 pm?
   3 On Wednesday she goes to bed at 2.15 pm?
   4 On Thursday she goes to bed at 2 pm?
   5 On Friday she goes to bed at 1.30 pm?

F Baby John has his first feed at 6 am and the
last one at 10 pm.
He has a feed every 4 hours.
When should he have the other feeds?

Pages from Joe's drawing book

BUS STOP

	am					am	then every 10 minutes	pm		then every 20 minutes	pm
Deepdene	7.02	7.22	7.42	8.02	8.22	8.32		6.12	6.32		10.32
Market Place	7.12	7.32	7.52	8.12	8.32	8.42		6.22	6.42		10.42
King's Head	7.19	7.39	7.59	8.19	8.39	8.49		6.29	6.49		—

1 This part of the timetable shows that the first bus leaves Deepdene at 7.02 am.
It gets to the Market Place at . . . am and the King's Head at 7.19 am.

2 If you must reach the Market Place by 8.00 am, what time must you catch
the bus at Deepdene?

3 How long does the journey from the Market Place to the King's Head take?

4 When does the next bus after the 8.32 am leave Deepdene?
Write out some more of the bus times for yourself.

5 If you have to be in the Market Place at 11.00 am what time must you leave Deepdene?

	am					am	then every 10 minutes	pm		then every 20 minutes	pm
King's Head	7.03	7.23	7.43	8.03	8.23	8.33		6.13	6.33		10.33
Market Place	7.10	7.30	7.50	8.10	8.30	8.40		6.20	6.40		10.40
Deepdene	7.20	7.40	8.00	8.20	8.40	8.50		6.30	6.50		—

6 What time does the first bus leave the King's Head?
How long does it take to reach the Market Place?

7 If you are at the King's Head and have to get to Deepdene by 9.00 am
which bus must you catch?

8 If you have to be at the Market Place by 3.00 pm, which bus do you
catch from the King's Head?

Deepdene

22 p	Woodland Road			
22 p	22 p	Station Road		
23 p	22 p	22 p	Market Place	
23 p	23 p	23 p	22 p	Park Road
23 p	23 p	23 p	23 p	22 p	King's Head

9 The table shows that the fare from Woodland Road to the Market Place is 22 p.
What is the fare from Deepdene to the Market Place?
What is the fare from Park Road to Deepdene?

10 If you live near the King's Head and go to the Market Place twice on
Saturday, how much will it cost you if you use the bus for each journey?

EAT IT UP

By what date must these be eaten?

1

Cream
Eat within
3 days

Date of Purchase

Thursday
14th March

2

Yoghurt
Use in 4 days

Wednesday
19th June

3

Fruit cake
Eat within
3 weeks

Tuesday
1st November

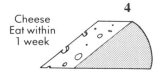

4

Cheese
Eat within
1 week

Monday
23rd September

5

Sausages
Eat within 2 days

Monday
17th December

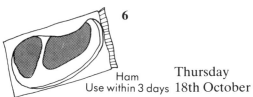

6

Ham
Use within 3 days

Thursday
18th October

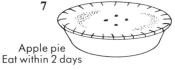

7

Apple pie
Eat within 2 days

Saturday
20th March

8

Strawberry
flan
Eat on day
of purchase

Friday
24th July

9

Jam Tarts
Eat within 2 days

Date of Purchase

Tuesday
17th May

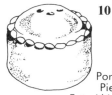

10

Pork
Pie
Eat within 1 day

Friday
11th April

11

Bacon
Use within 4 days

Wednesday
8th August

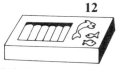

12

Fish Fingers
Eat within 2 days

Tuesday
16th June

13

Chicken Pie
Use within 1 day

Friday
12th November

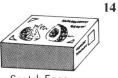

14

Scotch Eggs
Use within 2 days

Wednesday
16th March

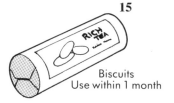

15

Biscuits
Use within 1 month

Friday
10th April

CATCHING THE BUS

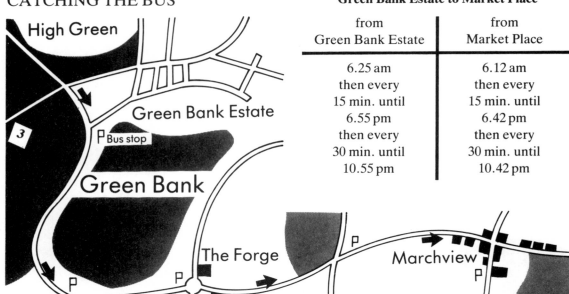

Green Bank Estate to Market Place	
from Green Bank Estate	from Market Place
6.25 am then every 15 min. until 6.55 pm then every 30 min. until 10.55 pm	6.12 am then every 15 min. until 6.42 pm then every 30 min. until 10.42 pm

A Ann lives on the Green Bank Estate.
She must leave home 5 minutes before the bus goes.
When must she leave the house to catch these buses:
1 8.25 am   **2** 3.10 pm   **3** 7.25 pm?

B The journey from town takes 10 minutes.
When will Ann get home if

1 on Monday she catches the bus at 4.12 pm?
2 on Tuesday she catches the bus at 4.27 pm?
3 on Wednesday she catches the bus at 5.12 pm?
4 on Thursday she catches the bus at 12.57 pm?
5 on Friday she catches the bus at 5.42 pm?

C Ann must go to town for these times. When must she
leave her house?
The bus journey takes 10 minutes.

1 Monday: Dentist at 10.30 am
2 Tuesday: Youth Club at 8.00 pm
3 Wednesday: meet Joan at 3.00 pm
4 Friday: Hairdresser at 2.15 pm

D **1** What is the earliest Ann can be in town?
2 When does the last bus leave town?
3 If Ann catches the last bus, when will she get home?

Bus route

54

TELEVISION VIEWING

Pie chart for Friday evening 5 pm–11 pm on BBC 1

1 What kind of programme took most time?
2 How many minutes are represented on the chart for Friday?
3 How many minutes will one degree represent?

4 Children's TV lasted 50 minutes. Measure the angle.
5 On Friday, how much time is given
    (a) to news?
    (b) to Westerns?
    (c) to detective stories?

6 On which day was more time given to news?
7 How much longer did the Western last on Saturday than Friday?
8 Draw a pie chart of television viewing on Saturday evening.
9 Compare these figures with those of other channels.

Saturday evening	5 pm–11 pm
Sport	105 minutes
Cartoons	30 minutes
News	25 minutes
Science fiction	25 minutes
Westerns	80 minutes
Comedy	45 minutes
Detective stories	50 minutes

THE CALENDAR

A 1 Today is Friday 14th September.   What day is 18th September?

2 Today is Thursday 9th January.   What day is 12th January?

3 Today is Saturday 23rd August.   What day is 30th August?

4 Today is Monday 11th December.   What day is 14th December?

5 Today is Thursday 24th March.   What day was 22nd March?

6 Today is Friday 11th February.   What day was 10th February?

7 Today is Tuesday 15th October.   What day was 10th October?

8 Today is Sunday 5th April.   What day was 1st April?

9 Today is Monday 25th January.   What was last Friday's date?

10 Today is Thursday 9th March.   What was last Monday's date?

11 Today is Saturday 23rd June.   What was last Saturday's date?

12 Today is Tuesday 6th February.   What was last Sunday's date?

13 Today is Monday 10th June.   What will be Friday's date?

14 Today is Wednesday 8th August.   What will be Saturday's date?

15 Today is Saturday 18th May.   What will be next Saturday's date?

16 Today is Friday 8th October.   What will be Monday's date?

JULY						
Sun	Mon	Tue	Wed	Thu	Fri	Sat
						1
2	3	4	5	6	7	8
9	10	11	12	13	14	15
16	17	18	19	20	21	22
23	24	25	26	27	28	29
30	31					

B 1 What day is 11th July? How many days is it after 4th July?

2 Today is Monday 10th July. What will it be next Monday?

3 What will be the date one week after Thursday 20th July?

4 What was the date two weeks before Wednesday 26th July?

5 Write down the dates of all the Saturdays.

6 In another month Tuesday is the 2nd. Write down the dates of the other Tuesdays in that month.

7 Pat was absent from the 10th to the 14th. How many days was she absent?

8 John was absent from the 18th to 21st. How many days was he absent?

9 What day is the 30th June?

10 What day is 1st August?

11 area

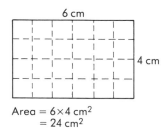

Area = 6×4 cm²
    = 24 cm²

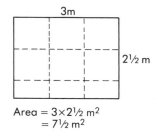

Area of shaded part
= 60−21 cm²
= 39 cm²

Area = 3×2½ m²
    = 7½ m²

A Find the area of these rectangles:

	length	breadth
1	3 cm	6 cm
2	4 cm	7 cm
3	2.5 cm	6 cm
4	5.7 cm	3 cm
5	6.7 cm	8 cm

B Find the area of the shaded part.

	Inner rectangle:		Outer rectangle:	
	length	breadth	length	breadth
1	2 cm	3 cm	4 cm	4 cm
2	3 cm	5 cm	4 cm	6 cm
3	4 cm	4 cm	7 cm	7 cm
4	4 cm	5.5 cm	9 cm	10 cm
5	6 cm	2.5 cm	8 cm	8 cm

C Find the area of these shapes:

1
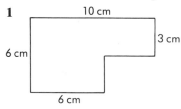

2
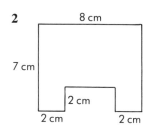

3
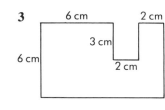

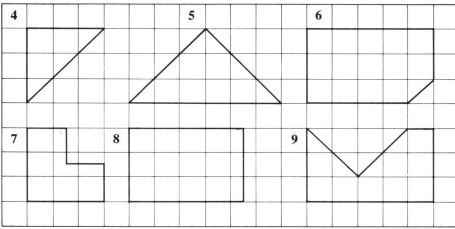

On this grid, each square represents 1 m².

57

A A rectangle has been drawn so as just to enclose this leaf.

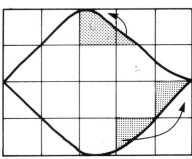

1 What is the area of this rectangle?
   Make a statement about the area of the leaf using the sign <.

2 How many complete 1 cm squares are within the leaf?
   Make another statement about the area of the leaf and those squares.

3 Use the results from 1 and 2 to complete this statement:
   ... < area of leaf < ...

4 There is no formula for finding the area of some shapes, so
   we count the number of squares they cover. Look at the leaf shape
   again. If a square is only partly covered, try to find a piece which could
   be moved to make a whole square. Two have already been done on this
   leaf.
   Do the rest yourself and find the area of the leaf.
   Does this result fit into the statement you made for 3?

5   Is more or less than half of this square shaded?
    An approximate answer for the area of the leaf can be found by
   counting the squares it covers and using the rule:
   (a) Count all the whole squares.
   (b) Count half a square, or more than half a square, as if it were a
       whole square.
   (c) Ignore the pieces which are less than half a square.
       What does this method give for the area of the leaf?

6 Which do you think is the best method for finding the area of an
   irregular shape like a leaf?

B Find the areas of these shapes. Each square represents 1 in^2.

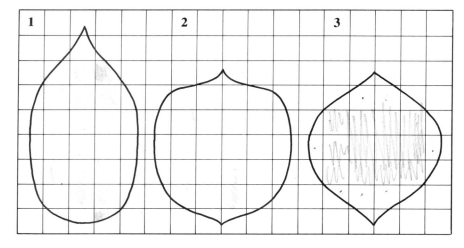

EXAMPLE

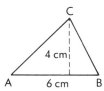

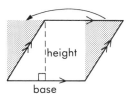

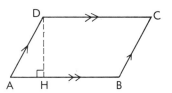

Area of triangle = $\frac{1}{2}$ base × height

e.g. Area △ ABC = $\frac{1}{2}$ 6 × 4 cm²

$\qquad$ = 12 cm²

Area of a parallelogram = base × perpendicular height.

e.g. AB = 5 cm, DH = 4 cm;

area of ABCD = 5 × 4 = 20 cm²

A

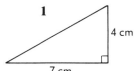

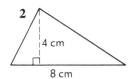

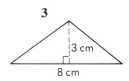

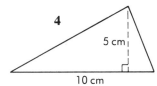

Copy each triangle and draw the rectangle which just encloses the triangle.

Mark the measurements of the rectangle and calculate its area. Find the area of each triangle.

B Calculate the area of these triangles:

	base	perpendicular height		base	perpendicular height
1	4 cm	3 cm	11	16 cm	8 cm
2	3 cm	6 cm	12	15 cm	18 cm
3	4 cm	6 cm	13	20 cm	16.7 cm
4	6 cm	4.2 cm	14	7.8 cm	10 cm
5	6 cm	9 cm	15	4.6 cm	5 cm
6	5 cm	7 cm	16	6 cm	5.6 cm
7	12 cm	7 cm	17	8.2 cm	10 cm
8	7 cm	8 cm	18	4.6 cm	6 cm
9	15 cm	8 cm	19	6.3 cm	10 cm
10	14 cm	12 cm	20	16 cm	15.4 cm

C Calculate the area of these parallelograms:

	base	perpendicular height		base	perpendicular height
1	5 cm	6 cm	11	4 cm	7.5 cm
2	13 cm	10 cm	12	6 cm	7.8 cm
3	20 cm	15 cm	13	14 cm	6 cm
4	3.4 cm	5 cm	14	15 cm	6.8 cm
5	6.5 cm	4 cm	15	20 cm	14.5 cm
6	4.8 cm	5 cm	16	23 cm	10.6 cm
7	6.7 cm	6 cm	17	16 cm	13.6 cm
8	23 cm	20 cm	18	12 cm	7 cm
9	7 cm	8.6 cm	19	5.6 cm	7.8 cm
10	30 cm	25 cm	20	8.9 cm	4.6 cm

WALLS AND CEILINGS

A These diagrams show the walls of a room with its windows and doors.
Calculate the area of the part of each wall which would have to be painted.
What is the total wall area to be painted?

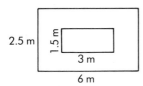 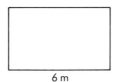

B Make a sketch of the ceiling of each of these rooms and calculate its area.

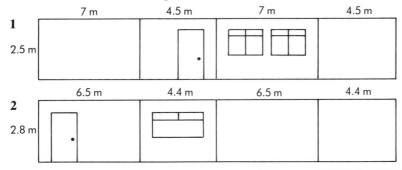

C Calculate the area of these walls to be painted.

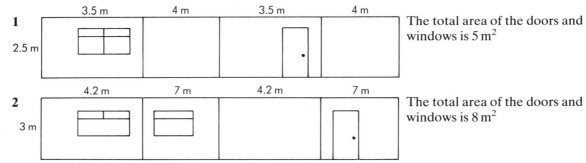

1 The total area of the doors and windows is 5 m²

2 The total area of the doors and windows is 8 m²

D The walls and ceiling of these rooms have to be painted with the same emulsion paint.
What is the total surface to be covered?

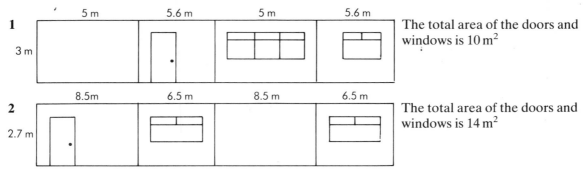

1 The total area of the doors and windows is 10 m²

2 The total area of the doors and windows is 14 m²

AREA OF THE CIRCLE

$\pi = 3.14$ to 2 decimal places.
$\pi = 3.1$ to 1 decimal place.

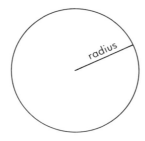

The area of a circle is πr^2
e.g. If the radius is 4 cm
$$\text{Area} = \pi \times 4 \times 4 \, \text{cm}^2$$
$$= 3.14 \times 4 \times 4 \, \text{cm}^2$$
$$= 50.24 \, \text{cm}^2$$

A Find the area of these circles.
Use $\pi = 3.1$.

Give the answer correct to 1 decimal place.

1	radius = 3 cm	**11**	radius = 8.4 cm
2	radius = 5 cm	**12**	radius = 3.5 cm
3	radius = 4 cm	**13**	radius = 9.5 cm
4	radius = 6 cm	**14**	radius = 12 cm
5	radius = 1 cm	**15**	radius = 6.8 cm
6	radius = 10 cm	**16**	radius = 20 cm
7	radius = 2 cm	**17**	radius = 4.5 cm
8	radius = 8 cm	**18**	radius = 3.9 cm
9	radius = 2.5 cm	**19**	radius = 7.1 cm
10	radius = 6.6 cm	**20**	radius = 1.1 cm

B Find the area of these circles.
Use $\pi = 3.14$.

Give the answer correct to 2 decimal places.

1	radius = 2 cm	**11**	radius = 4.8 cm
2	radius = 4 cm	**12**	radius = 15 cm
3	radius = 5 cm	**13**	radius = 7.6 cm
4	radius = 3.5 cm	**14**	radius = 8.2 cm
5	radius = 6.1 cm	**15**	radius = 16.4 cm
6	radius = 7.2 cm	**16**	radius = 8.6 cm
7	radius = 8.4 cm	**17**	radius = 9.2 cm
8	radius = 3.9 cm	**18**	radius = 30 cm
9	radius = 8.6 cm	**19**	radius = 28 cm
10	radius = 5.5 cm	**20**	radius = 27 cm

Approximating to check the use of a calculator

Example

Find the area of a circle of radius 5.1 cm.
Checking:
$\pi > 3$, $5.1 > 5$, so $r^2 > 25$ and $\pi r^2 > 3 \times 25$
The answer should be greater than 75 cm².

C Find an approximate value for each of these before using a calculator
to find the area of these circles.
Use $\pi = 3.14$

1	radius = 4.1 cm	**6**	radius = 7.2 cm
2	radius = 5.2 cm	**7**	radius = 6.2 cm
3	radius = 7.3 cm	**8**	radius = 10.3 cm
4	radius = 3.1 cm	**9**	radius = 10.2 cm
5	radius = 3.3 cm	**10**	radius = 6.3 cm

12 3-D thinking and volume

WRAPPERS

A

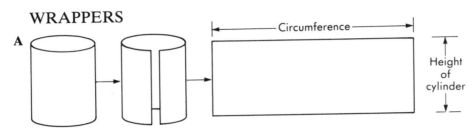

A paper wrapper is to be made for each of these cylinders. It has to cover the sides completely so 1 cm is allowed for overlap of the edges to be joined.
Make a sketch of the paper to be cut for each wrapper and show its measurements.
Calculate the area of each wrapper.

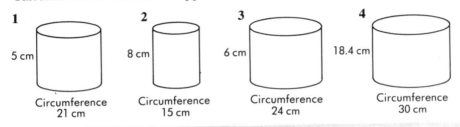

1
5 cm
Circumference
21 cm

2
8 cm
Circumference
15 cm

3
6 cm
Circumference
24 cm

4
18.4 cm
Circumference
30 cm

B This box is to be covered completely with paper. No overlaps are
needed. The diagram shows the shape of the paper which is to be used.
Make a copy of it and mark the length of each edge.

The shape is cut from a rectangle of
paper. What are its measurements?
What is the area of this rectangle?
Calculate the area of the paper which
is wasted.

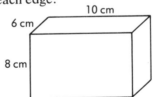

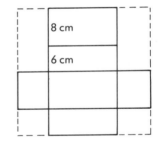

C These boxes have to be covered in
the same way as the one above.
What are the measurements of the
rectangle of paper needed for
each box?
Choose the plan for each box which
wastes least paper.

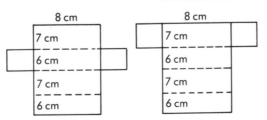

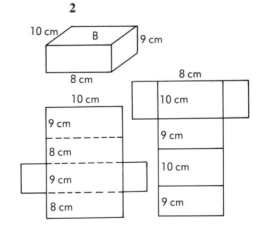

STACKING BOXES

A A lorry brings a grocer 24 boxes of tinned meat.

To make more room he stacks them in his cellar.
First he makes a layer, 3 boxes long and 2 wide.

1 How many boxes are there in this layer?

2 Then he puts another layer on top of this one.
How many boxes has he used altogether?

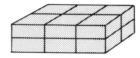

3 How many layers will he need to stack all the 24 boxes?

4 If he had a lot of boxes to stack and used a bottom layer 4 boxes long
and 5 wide, how many would there be in this layer?

5 If he had 2 layers, how many boxes would he have stacked?

6 If he had 3 layers, how many boxes would he have stacked?

B Copy and complete the following table.

	Number of boxes long	Number of boxes wide	Number of layers	Total number of boxes
	4	5	4	80
	6	5	3	90
1	5	4	6	
2	4	6	2	
3	8	5	3	
4	6	3	2	
5	6	3	5	
6	4	5	6	

MODELS

P folds up to make s.

Write P → s.

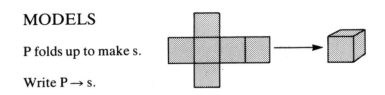

When these shapes are cut and folded, which solids do they form?
Make a list, showing the name of each solid, for example A → s, cone.

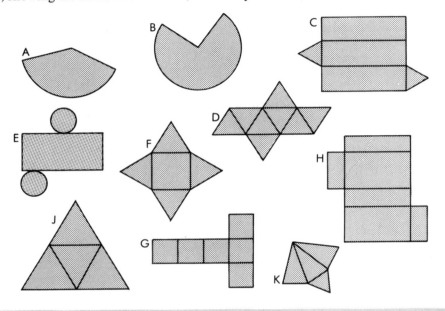

Solids

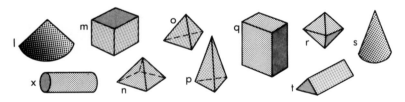

triangular prism	cylinder	rectangular block
octahedron	tetrahedron	pyramid on a square base
cone	cube	pyramid on a triangular base

THE FIVE REGULAR SOLIDS

Tetrahedron

Cube

Octahedron

Dodecahedron

Icosahedron

A 1 Each face of a cube is a square.

How many faces has a cube?
How many corners has a cube?
How many edges has a cube?

2 Each face of a tetrahedron is a triangle.

How many faces has a tetrahedron?
How many corners has a tetrahedron?
How many edges has a tetrahedron?

3 Count the faces, corners and edges of the other solids in the same way.
The diagram shows the front part of the dodecahedron. The unseen part also has six faces.
Perhaps you can find an object with this shape, e.g. some paperweights.

4 Copy your results on to a table like the one below.
Add the number of faces to the number of corners and put the result in the fifth column.
Compare the fourth and fifth columns.
What do you notice?

	Faces	Corners	Edges	Faces + Corners
Tetrahedron				
Cube				
Octahedron				
Dodecahedron	12			
Icosahedron	20			

B Which of these nets will form a cube?

1

2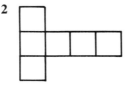

3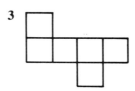

4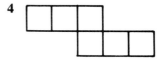

5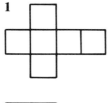

6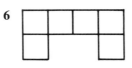

7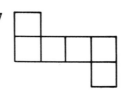

For a solid with a uniform cross-section: Volume = area of cross-section × length

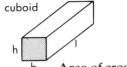

cuboid

Area of cross-section = $h \times b$
Volume of cuboid = $h \times b \times l$

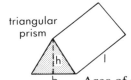

triangular prism

Area of cross-section = $\frac{1}{2} b \times h$
Volume of triangular prism = $\frac{1}{2} b \times h \times l$

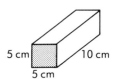

5 cm   10 cm
5 cm

Area of
cross-section $= 5 \times 5 \text{ cm}^2$
$\qquad = 25 \text{ cm}^2$
Volume $= 25 \times 10 \text{ cm}^3$
$\qquad = 250 \text{ cm}^3$

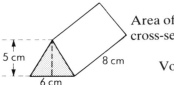

5 cm   8 cm
6 cm

Area of
cross-section $= \frac{1}{2} \times 6 \times 5 \text{ cm}^2$
$\qquad = 15 \text{ cm}^2$
Volume $= 15 \times 8 \text{ cm}^3$
$\qquad = 120 \text{ cm}^3$

A Calculate the volume of these cuboids:

cross-section	length
1 6 cm^2	10 cm
2 4 cm^2	6 cm
3 2 cm by 3 cm	5 cm
4 1.5 cm by 4 cm	10 cm
5 4 cm by 2.5 cm	8 cm
6 8 cm^2	12 cm
7 16 cm^2	9 cm
8 5 cm by 6 cm	18 cm
9 7 cm by 5 cm	9 cm
10 8 cm by 6 cm	12 cm
11 6 cm^2	5 cm
12 8 cm^2	3 cm
13 3 cm by 2 cm	7 cm
14 5 cm by 2 cm	8.6 cm
15 4 cm by 2.5 cm	9.8 cm

B Calculate the volume of these triangular prisms:

cross-section	length
1 7.5 cm^2	8 cm
2 12.4 cm^2	6 cm
3 3.8 cm^2	9 cm
4 5.7 cm^2	7 cm
5 9.4 cm^2	6 cm
6 5 cm^2	5.5 cm
7 4 cm^2	12 cm
8 6.1 cm^2	5 cm
9 4.2 cm^2	6 cm
10 6 cm^2	4.3 cm

base	height	length
11 2 cm	by 3 cm	5 cm
12 1.5 cm	by 4 cm	10 cm
13 4 cm	by 2.5 cm	8 cm
14 7 cm	by 5 cm	9 cm
15 8 cm	by 6 cm	12 cm

C The volume of each small brick is 3 cm^3.
What is the volume of these shapes?

1

2

13 charts and plans

A These charts show the average temperature for each month in °F.

1 Where would you find the highest temperature in February?
2 Which is the coolest month in Brazil?
3 Which shows least change of temperature throughout the year?
4 For how many months is the average temperature in Bermuda below 70 °F?

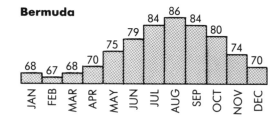

Bermuda

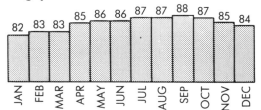

Singapore

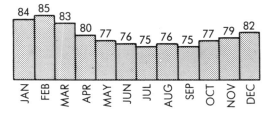

Brazil

B These charts show the temperatures and hours of sunshine.

1 Which are the hottest months in Tunisia?
2 Which are the hottest months in the Algarve?

3 When could you expect 12 or more hours of sunshine in the Algarve?

Tunisia	Average max. day time temp.	Average max. hours of sunshine
APR	69° F	7.8
MAY	77° F	10.0
JUN	84° F	11.0
JUL	90° F	12.2
AUG	90° F	11.2
SEP	85° F	8.6
OCT	77° F	7.3
NOV	69° F	6.2

Algarve	Average max. day time temp.	Average max. hours of sunshine
APR	67° F	9.2
MAY	71° F	10.2
JUN	77° F	12.0
JUL	83° F	12.2
AUG	83° F	11.6
SEP	78° F	9.3
OCT	72° F	7.6
NOV	65° F	6.0

C This chart shows the monthly averages of the weather conditions in Lanzarote.

1 Which is the sunniest month?
2 In which month would you find the highest temperatures?
3 Which are the hottest months in London?
4 When is the biggest difference between the temperatures in London and Lanzarote?

	APR	MAY	JUN	JUL	AUG	SEP	OCT
SUN HRS	8	10	11	12	11	9	7

AVERAGE DAILY MAXIMUM: 55 60 65 70 75 80 85 90 95

LONDON   LANZAROTE

D Which of these weather charts is easiest to read? Which gives most information?

THERMOMETERS

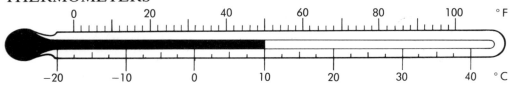

A The temperature shown on this thermometer can be read as 10 °C or 50 °F.
Use the thermometer as a conversion chart.

1 Convert these to °C

  85 °F   0 °F   32 °F   68 °F   98 °F

2 Convert these to °F

  0 °C   35 °C   25 °C   −10 °C   −5 °C

B When Jenny was ill her temperature was taken and the readings shown on a graph.

1 Which day was her temperature highest?
2 When did her temperature first drop back to normal?
3 Which day did her temperature begin to stay about normal?

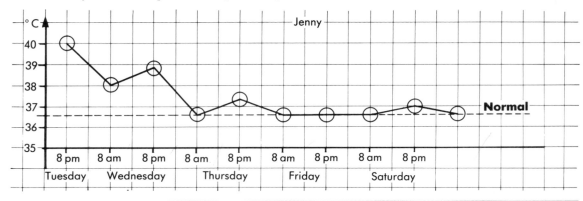

C

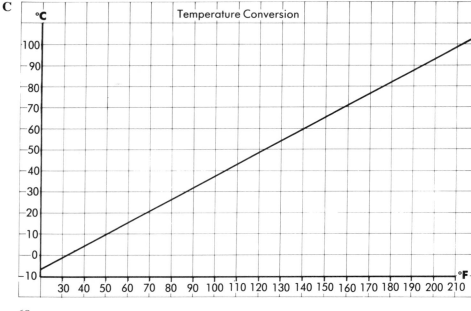

Use this graph to make these conversions:

1 60 °F to °C
2 50 °C to °F
3 20 °C to °F
4 −10 °C to °F
5 100 °F to °C
6 150 °F to °C
7 80 °F to °C
8 200 °F to °C
9 10 °C to °F
10 25 °C to °F

TEMPERATURE

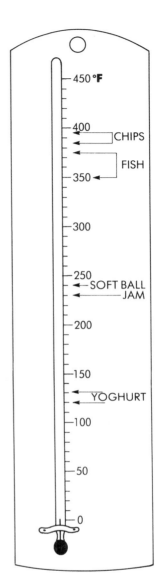

A 1 Mrs Smith is making strawberry jam.
How hot should it be?

2 Kathy knows that to make good chips they must be put into hot fat.
What temperature range does this thermometer show for making chips?

3 What is the lowest temperature for frying fish?

4 Ann is making some sweets. The recipe says the sugar must be heated to 240 °F.
What is this temperature called?

5 Yoghurt can be made at home. It has to be left standing in a warm place to make it set properly.
How warm should this place be?

B Mary wants to use some recipes from an old cookery book which gives numbers called N for the oven setting. There is a formula for changing those numbers into °F. When she uses this formula she can set her own oven temperature.
It is: temperature in °F $= 50 \times N + 220$, where N is the oven setting.

1 What temperature is needed for a cherry cake to be baked at oven setting 3?

2 The Christmas cake needs oven setting 2 for $1\frac{1}{2}$ hours and then oven setting 1 for a further 4 hours. What are the corresponding temperatures in °F?

3 How long will it take to cook the Christmas cake?

4 The recipe for puff pastry needs oven setting 5. How hot is this in °F?

C 1 This shows the formula for changing from X°C to °F: $\dfrac{9X}{5} + 32$

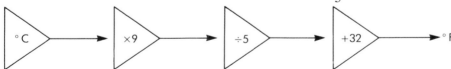

Use it to change these to °F: 30 °C, 100 °C, 60 °C, 45 °C, 0 °C.

2 Copy this and complete it to show how Y°F is changed to °C: $(Y - 32) \times \dfrac{5}{9}$

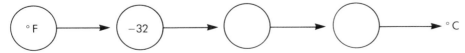

Use it to change these to °C: 122 °F, 41 °F, 59 °F, 212 °F, 32 °F.

TILES

A 1 How many tiles 30 cm
long would you need to
go along a wall
90 cm long?
120 cm long?
150 cm long?
210 cm long?
330 cm long?
600 cm long?
630 cm long?

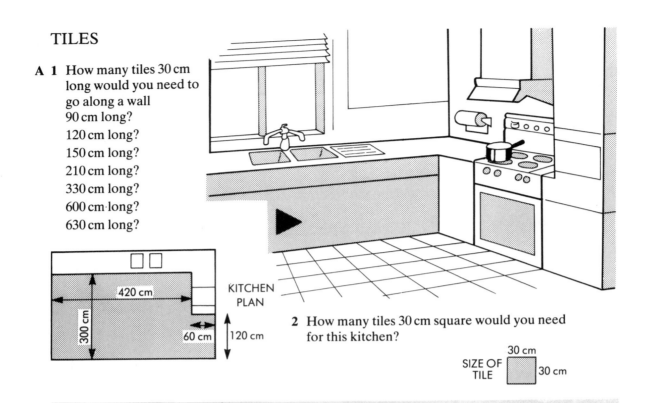

KITCHEN
PLAN

2 How many tiles 30 cm square would you need
for this kitchen?

SIZE OF
TILE

30 cm

30 cm

B 1 How many tiles 30 cm by 30 cm
would you need for an area
90 cm by 90cm?
60 cm by 60 cm?
120 cm by 150 cm?
210 cm by 300 cm?
150 cm by 600 cm?

30 cm

30 cm

2 How many tiles would you need
for this floor?

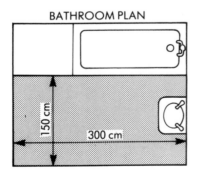

BATHROOM PLAN

150 cm

300 cm

C 1 If tiles are 50 cm square, how many tiles
would you need to cover an area
100 cm by 200 cm?   250 cm by 350 cm?
200 cm by 300 cm?   400 cm by 350 cm?
300 cm by 400 cm?

LIVING ROOM PLAN
400 cm

2 How many tiles
would you need
for this living
room?

50 cm

50 cm

SIZE OF TILE

700 cm

300 cm

650 cm

ROAD MAP

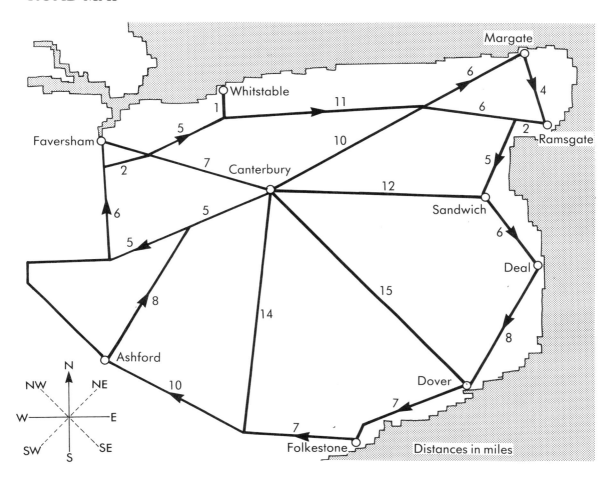

Margate

Whitstable

6

4

11

6

Faversham

5

10

2

Ramsgate

7

Canterbury

5

2

12

Sandwich

6

5

5

15

Deal

8

8

N

NW   NE

Ashford

10

W——E

SW   SE

S

14

Dover

7

7

8

Folkestone

Distances in miles

1 How many towns are named on the map?

2 How far is Canterbury from Deal by the shortest route?

3 How far is it from Whitstable to Margate?

4 How far is it from Ashford to Margate?

5 Which town is due south west of Canterbury?

6 How many towns are east of Canterbury?

7 Starting at Ramsgate and following the arrows, which is the first town you reach?

8 Following the arrows how long is the complete journey?

9 Going from Folkestone to Margate, how much shorter is it if you go through Deal rather than Canterbury?

10 If you had to build a direct road from Whitstable to Canterbury, how long do you think it would have to be?

11 In which direction would you travel from Dover to Canterbury?
It took $\frac{1}{2}$ hour to drive from Dover to Canterbury. What was the average speed?

12 A journey from Canterbury to Margate took 20 minutes. What was the average speed for this journey?

TRAVELLING

	EDINBURGH	EXETER	GLASGOW	LIVERPOOL	MANCHESTER	NEWCASTLE	YORK	LONDON
713								
69	716							
342	379	346						
341	381	342	52					
170	584	231	247	209				
297	468	336	154	103	130			
606	273	634	315	294	497	318		

The table shows the distance between towns measured in kilometres.
Check that it says:
Glasgow is 342 km from Manchester,
York is 297 km from Edinburgh.

1 How far is Edinburgh from Newcastle?
How far is Exeter from London?
How far is Liverpool from York?
How far is Manchester from Exeter?
How far is Edinburgh from Glasgow?

2 A man drives from London to York then on to Liverpool and straight back to London. How far does he travel?

3 Find the total length of these journeys:
London → Manchester → Newcastle → London
Edinburgh → Liverpool → London
Exeter → London → Exeter
Edinburgh → York → Manchester → Edinburgh

4 A car uses about four litres of petrol for every 50 km.
How much fuel would be used for each of these journeys:
London to Edinburgh?
Manchester to Glasgow?

5 A man plans to drive from York to Liverpool, then on to Exeter at an average speed of 60 km per hour. He allows 2½ hours for stops, how long should the journey take?

B A woman needs to reach the centre of Town A by 4.00 pm from Town B.

The air fare is £90 and the flight takes 1¼ hours. Passengers have to check in ½ hour before departure. The flight leaves at 1.15 pm.

The train fare is £60 and the journey takes 3 hours. There is a train at 1.00 pm.

It costs £14 for the petrol to drive a car from A to B and the driving time is 5 hours.

The bus fare is £35 and the journey takes 5½ hours including stops. It is scheduled to leave at 9.30 am.

Which means of transport should she choose and why?

GOING FROM PLACE TO PLACE

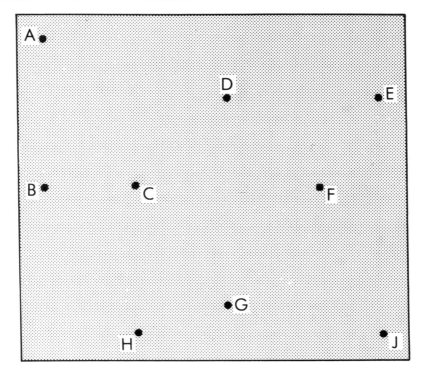

This map shows just the initial letters of the
place names. Scale: 4 mm = 1 km

This chart shows the shortest distance by road
from town to town. Check that it shows:
A is 13 km from D   B is 23 km from E.

A								
10	B							
	6	C						
13		9	D					
23	23	17	10	E				
21	18	12	9	7	F			
22	15		14	17	10	G		
21	12	10		23	16	7	H	
30	25	19	19	16	11	11		J

1 Use the chart to find how far it is between these places:
   B and F   D and G   H and B   J and D.

2 Use the scale on the map to find these distances:
   A to C   B to D   C to G   H to J   D to H.

3 Which places are more than 25 km apart?

4 How far does a man travel when he goes from A to B and then to G and back to A?

5 How far does a boy cycle when he goes from E to F to D and back to E?

6 A boy can cycle 20 km in an hour. How long does it take to go from C to G?

73

14 angles and shape

VIEW POINT

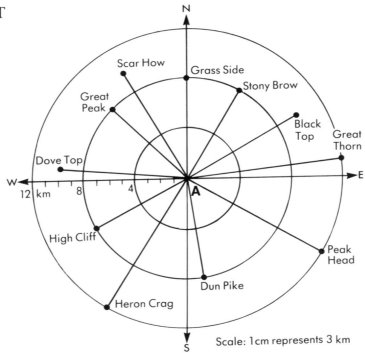

Scale: 1cm represents 3 km

The diagram shows the hills which can be seen from point A.

1 Looking North, Grass Side is 8 km away.
   Scar How is 10 km away.
   How many hills are more than 8 km from A?

2 Standing at A looking North, turn slowly
   through 30° towards the East.
   Stony Brow can now be seen. It is N30°E
   from A. How far away is Stony Brow?

3 Look North again and turn to face N60°E.
   Which hill can be seen?

4 When facing N80°E which hill can be seen?

5 Copy and complete this table:

Direction	Name of hill	Distance from A
S10°E S30°W	Dun Pike	
	High Cliff Great Peak Peak Head	

6 Make a scale drawing showing A, High Cliff
   and Heron Crag.
   Let 1 cm represent 1 km.
   Use the drawing to find the distance from
   Heron Crag to High Cliff.

7 Make a scale drawing showing A, Peak Head
   and Great Thorn.
   Use it to find the distance
   between Peak Head and Great Thorn.

8 Use a scale drawing to find the distance
   between Stony Brow and Great Peak.

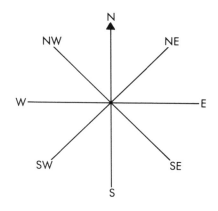

A How many degrees will the minute hand turn in:

1	1 hour	**6**	45 minutes
2	Half an hour	**7**	30 minutes
3	Quarter of an hour	**8**	40 minutes
4	10 minutes	**9**	50 minutes
5	20 minutes	**10**	5 minutes

Say how many degrees the hour hand will turn through in:

11	12 hours	**16**	$\frac{1}{2}$ hour
12	6 hours	**17**	3 hours
13	1 hour	**18**	9 hours
14	5 hours	**19**	$\frac{1}{4}$ hour
15	7 hours	**20**	$\frac{3}{4}$ hour

B Face north and turn clockwise, then say which direction you are facing when you have turned:

1	90°	**5**	135°
2	180°	**6**	270°
3	45°	**7**	225°
4	315°	**8**	360°

Face south. Say how many degrees you have to turn clockwise to face:

9	West	**12**	East
10	South-west	**13**	North
11	North-west	**14**	South-east

Face east. Say how many degrees you need to turn clockwise to face:

15	South-east	**18**	West
16	North-west	**19**	South-west
17	South	**20**	North

C Sketch a clock face to show each of these times.
Then calculate the angle between the hands at each time.

1	6.00 pm	**7**	5.40 pm
2	6.30 pm	**8**	1.20 pm
3	4.15 pm	**9**	2.40 pm
4	8.30 pm	**10**	3.50 pm
5	3.45 pm	**11**	7.15 pm
6	4.40 pm	**12**	1.30 am

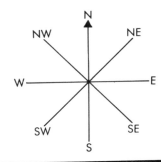

A man standing at P and looking towards Q is facing NE

Q

P

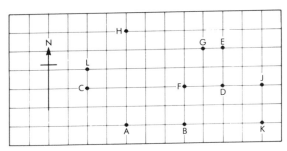

A Say in which direction a man is looking when he is

1 standing at A looking towards K
2 standing at A looking towards H
3 standing at H looking towards A
4 standing at C looking towards L
5 standing at D looking towards J
6 standing at D looking towards F
7 standing at E looking towards F
8 standing at F looking towards H
9 standing at E looking towards G
10 standing at J looking towards E

11 standing at F looking towards D
12 standing at D looking towards K
13 standing at F looking towards B
14 standing at K looking towards D
15 standing at F looking towards E
16 standing at H looking towards F
17 standing at B looking towards D
18 standing at J looking towards D
19 standing at K looking towards B
20 standing at H looking towards L

B The diagram shows a lighthouse L and the pier P.

1 Use a protractor to find the direction of the lighthouse from the pier.
2 A lifeboat sets out from the pier to reach a ship in distress at S. The lifeboat heads due North for 6 miles before turning westwards. How far does it travel from the pier to the ship?
3 The maximum speed is 30 mph. How soon can it possibly reach the ship?

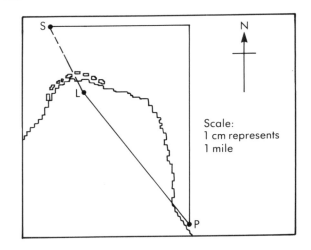

Scale:
1 cm represents
1 mile

EXAMPLES

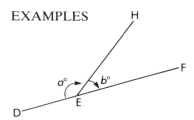

∠ DEH and ∠ HEF make a straight line:
$a° + b° = 180°$

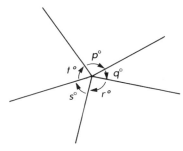

$p° + q° + r° + s° + t° = 360°$
$p° + q° + r° + s° + t°$ make a complete turn.

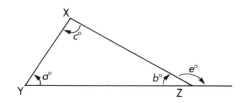

The angles of a triangle add up to 180°:
$a° + b° + c° = 180°$
∠ XZV is the exterior angle of the triangle:
$e° = a° + c°$

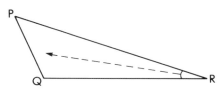

In this △, ∠ R is the smallest ∠ . It is opposite to
the shortest side, PQ.
∠ Q is the largest angle
and is opposite to the longest side, PR.

A QOS is a straight line.
Calculate the size of:

1 ∠ SOP
2 ∠ ROP
3 ∠ ROQ
4 ∠ TOP

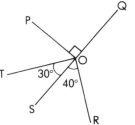

XY and AB are straight lines. Calculate the
size of:

5 ∠ AOK
6 ∠ AOY
7 ∠ BOY
8 ∠ XOB
9 ∠ AOX
10 ∠ KOX

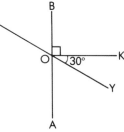

B
1 If $a = 40°$, $b = 60°$, find c. Which is the longest side?
2 If $a = 50°$, $b = 65°$, find c. Which is the shortest side?
3 If $a = 35°$, $b = 70°$, find c. Which is the shortest side?
4 If $b = 80°$, $c = 30°$, find a. Which is the longest side?
5 If $a = 55°$, $b = 75°$, find c. Which is the shortest side?
6 If $b = 84°$, $c = 42°$, find a. Which is the longest side?
7 If $a = 47°$, $b = 90°$, find c. Which is the longest side?
8 If $a = b$, $c = 80°$, find a and b.
9 If $b = 130°$, $a = c$, find a and c.
10 If $c = 46°$, $b = 98°$, find a.
11 If $k = 85°$, find b.

12 If $b = 115°$, find k.
13 If $a = 55°$, $c = 60°$, find k.
14 If $c = 63°$, $a = 58°$, find k.
15 If $k = 105°$, $a = 63°$, find c.

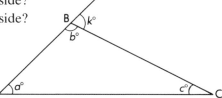

77

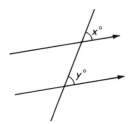

$x = y$

Corresponding angles on parallel lines

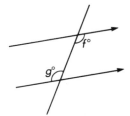

$f = g$

Alternate angles on parallel lines

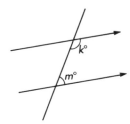

$m° + k° = 180°$

Interior angles on parallel lines

Copy the diagram, and mark the angle given, for each question.
Give a reason for each answer.

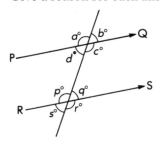

A **1** $a = 30°$; find b.
    2 $a = 40°$; find p.
    3 $q = 50°$; find c.
    4 $r = 120°$; find c.
    5 $s = 35°$; find d.
    6 $b = 40°$; find c.
    7 $d = 70°$; find q.
    8 $c = 135°$; find p.
    9 $c = 130°$; find q.
    10 $d = 50°$; find q.
    11 $q = 65°$; find b.
    12 $p = 105°$; find d.
    13 $c = 100°$; find q.
    14 $c = 145°$; find p.
    15 $d = 50°$; find p.

16 $d = 46°$; find q.
17 $b = 38°$; find q.
18 $p = 134°$; find c.
19 $r = 153°$; find c.
20 $p = 129°$; find a.

B **1** $a = 104°$; find s.
    2 $b = 64°$; find s.
    3 $d = 86°$; find p.
    4 $c = 93°$; find p.
    5 $r = 105°$; find b.
    6 $d = 98°$; find a.
    7 $c = 101°$; find p.
    8 $s = 107°$; find b.
    9 $q = 86°$; find c.
    10 $r = 87°$; find b.
    11 $q = 112°$; find d.
    12 $r = 84°$; find c.
    13 $a = 102°$; find p.
    14 $d = 109°$; find b.
    15 $s = 76°$; find b.

16 $p = 83°$; find a.
17 $q = 64°$; find c.
18 $a = 65°$; find s.
19 $d = 85°$; find r.
20 $a = 80°$; find p.

EXAMPLE

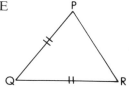

△ PQR is an isosceles triangle. ∠P = ∠R

△ DEF is isosceles.
$d = f$ and $d + f = 70°$
$d = 35°, f = 35°$

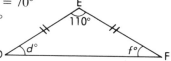

A Draw a new sketch for each question.

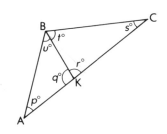

1 $p = 50°$, $q = 120°$; find u.
2 $u = 40°$, $t = 70°$; find $\angle ABC$.
3 $u = 35°$, $p = 49°$; find r.
4 $q = 107°$; find r.
5 $s = 38°$, $t = 84°$; find q.
6 $p = 40°$, $s = 54°$, $t = 43°$; find u.
7 $p = 56°$, $r = 134°$; find u.
8 $t = 82°$, $s = 24°$; find q.
9 $q = 140°$, $t = 68°$; find s.
10 $q = 119°$; find r.
11 $p = 45°$, $s = 45°$, what kind of angle is $\angle ABC$?
12 $r = 104°$, $t = 48°$; find s.
13 $r = 124°$, $u = 54°$; find p.
14 $p = 38°$, $u = 64°$, $s = 43°$; find t.
15 $q = 117°$; find r.
16 $p = u$, $r = 110°$; find p.
17 $r = t$, $s = 40°$; find q.
18 $t = 68°$, $s = 42°$; find q.
19 $\angle AKB = 105°$; find $\angle BKC$.
20 $AK = BK$, $\angle AKB = 120°$; find $\angle A$.

B Give reasons for each answer.

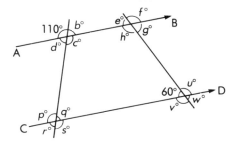

1 Find b.   6 Find g.
2 Find c.   7 Find q.
3 Find d.   8 Find u.
4 Find p.   9 Find r.
5 Find e.   10 Find w.

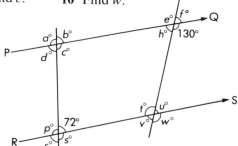

11 Find t.   16 Find d.
12 Find c.   17 Find u.
13 Find p.   18 Find b.
14 Find r.   19 Find f.
15 Find h.   20 Find a.

C Find, giving reasons:

1 $\angle DAB$.   5 $\angle ADE$.
2 $\angle ADC$.   6 $\angle DCA$.
3 $\angle ABC$.   7 $\angle EAD$.
4 $\angle ACB$.   8 $\angle AED$.

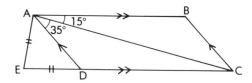

Find, giving reasons:

9 $\angle RPS$.   17 $\angle QSR$.   19 $\angle PQK$.
10 $\angle RPQ$.   18 $\angle QKR$.   20 $\angle RKS$.
11 $\angle SRP$.
12 $\angle PQR$.
13 $\angle PSR$.
14 $\angle RST$.
15 $\angle RQK$.
16 $\angle KSP$.

79

A Give the name of each shape, and the marked measurement.

1
30° ?

6
5 cm
?

11
?
105°

2
7 cm
?

12
?
65°

3
110°
?

7
50°
?

13
70°
?

4
80°
?

8
?

14
6 cm
?

5
70°
?

9
?

15
?

10
140°
?

B Calculate the size of:

1 ∠P   **2** ∠PQR   **3** ∠RSP   **4** ∠QSR

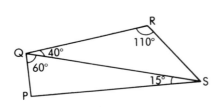

R
110°
Q 40°
60°
15° S
P

C Calculate the size of:

1 ∠QSR   **2** ∠RSP   **3** ∠PQS
4 ∠PQR

R
130°
Q 35°   S
80°
P

D Calculate the size of:

1 ∠CDB   **2** ∠BDA   **3** ∠ADC
4 ∠DBA

B
C
104°
BC‖AD
BC = CD
80°
A
D

E Calculate the size of:

1 ∠PSK **2** ∠QRK **3** ∠RQK **4** ∠QKP
5 ∠QPK **6** ∠QKP **7** ∠QPS **8** ∠RKS

Q
R
75°
K
40°
P
S
PS‖QR.
KP = KS

80

A Name the pair of congruent shapes in each of these figures. Make a list of the equal parts.

1

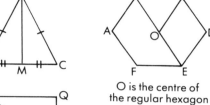

2

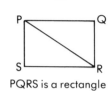

PQRS is a rectangle

3

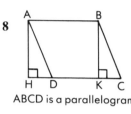

ABCD is a parallelogram

4

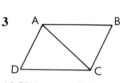

PQRS is a kite

5

ABC is an isosceles triangle

6

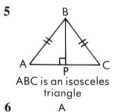

O is the centre of the circle

7

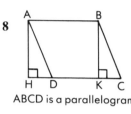

O is the centre of the regular hexagon

8

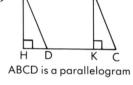

ABCD is a parallelogram

9

O is the centre of the regular pentagon ABCDE

10

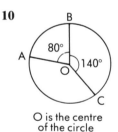

O is the centre of the circle

B Which of these pairs of shapes are congruent? If they are congruent show how they fit together, i.e. $\dfrac{ABC}{DFE}$ means A fits over D and AB fits over DF etc.

1

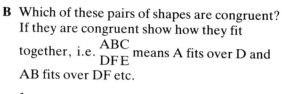

2

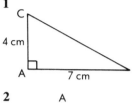 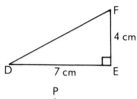

3

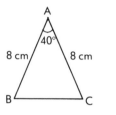 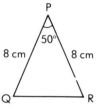

4

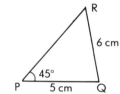

5

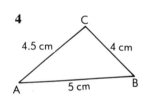 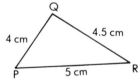

C Name the shapes which are congruent:

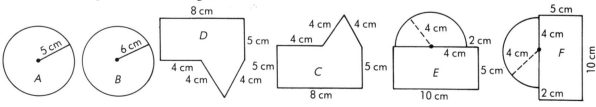

81

EXAMPLE

These shapes have line symmetry:

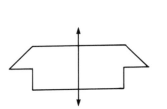 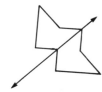

This shape has rotational symmetry:

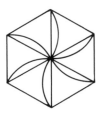

A Copy these shapes and the balance lines on squared paper. Complete them so they have line symmetry.

B This balance line goes through the corner of the squares. Complete them so they have line symmetry.

C Complete these shapes so they have rotational symmetry.

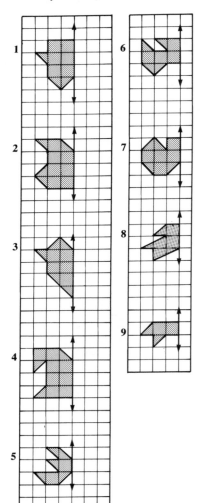 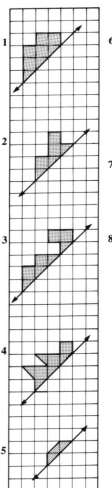 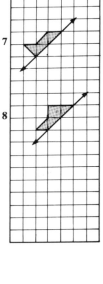 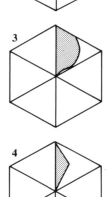

15 algebra

MACHINES

A Put 25p into a slot machine and you get a bar of chocolate.

This diagram shows what happens: 25p ——→ [_____] ——→ Chocolate

At the Post Office, put 50p in a slot machine and get a book of stamps. Draw a diagram to show what happens.

This machine multiplies numbers by . . .

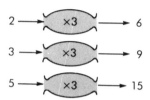

2 ——→ ×3 ——→ 6

3 ——→ ×3 ——→ 9

5 ——→ ×3 ——→ 15

B All these machines do things to numbers. Copy them and fill in the gaps. Notice that the machines are different shapes. One shape always does the same thing.

1
3 ——→ ×.. ——→15
8 ——→ ×.. ——→ 40
5 ——→ ×.. ——→ 25
6 ——→ ×.. ——→ ..

2
4 ——→ ×.. ——→ 16
6 ——→ ×.. ——→ 24
8 ——→ ×.. ——→ ..
27 ——→ ×.. ——→ ..

3
2 ——→ ×.. ——→ 22
5 ——→ ×.. ——→ 55
9 ——→ ×.. ——→ ..
k ——→ ×.. ——→ ..
p ——→ ×.. ——→ ..

4
2 ——→ ×.. ——→ 12
5 ——→ ×.. ——→ 30
8 ——→ ×.. ——→ ..
47 ——→ ×.. ——→ ..
h ——→ ×.. ——→

5
4 ——→ +.. ——→ 6
7 ——→ +.. ——→ 9
13 ——→ +.. ——→ ..
19 ——→ +.. ——→ ..
t ——→ +.. ——→ ..

6
8 ——→ ——→ 5
9 ——→ ——→ 6
13 ——→ ——→ 10
18 ——→ ——→ ..
N ——→ ——→

C Here the numbers have to go through two machines. The shape of these machines does not matter. Copy them and fill the gaps.

1
4 ——→ ×2 ——→ 8 ——→ ×3 ——→ 24
5 ——→ ×2 ——→ .. ——→ ×3 ——→ ..
3 ——→ ×6 ——→ .. ——→ +4 ——→ ..

2
6 ——→ ×9 ——→ .. ——→ +3 ——→ ..
11 ——→ −6 ——→ .. ——→ ×10 ——→ ..
10 ——→ ×3 ——→ .. ——→ −7 ——→ ..

Invent some machines of your own.

NOMOGRAMS

NB   You will probably find it easier to use a larger version of these
diagrams drawn on graph paper. A sheet of paper used as a straight edge
is more successful than a ruler for reading off results.

Make AB = BC.

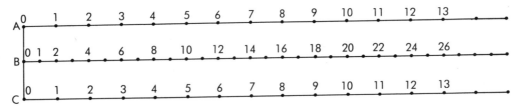

A Place a ruler on the lines above like this:
It joins 1 on A to 3 on C and passes through . . . on B.
The lines do the sum 1 + 3 = 4.

Now put the ruler to join 5 on A to 2 on C.
Where does it cross B? What sum is this?
Do more sums of this kind with the diagram.

Place the ruler on the lines like this:
It joins 6 on B to 4 on C and passes through . . . on A.
This does the sum 6 − 4 = . . .

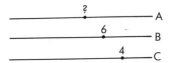

Now put the ruler to join 18 on B to 7 on C and it cuts A at . . .
These lines do sums like A + C, answer on B and like B − C, answer on A.

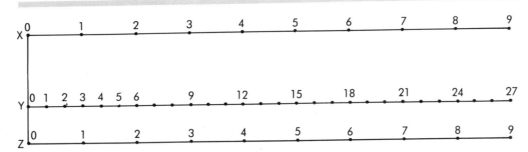

B Use the lines X, Y, Z. Notice that XY = 2YZ.
Join 8 on X to 5 on Z and it passes through . . . on Y; 8+ . . . ×5 = . . .
Join 7 on X to 3 on Z and it passes through . . . on Y; 7+ . . . ×3 = . . .
Use the diagram to do the following sums:
8 + 2 × 6 = . . . , 7 + 2 × 4 = . . . , 6 + 2 × 5 = . . . , 9 + 2 × 8 = . . .

These lines do sums like X + 2 × Z, answer on Y.

A Find the value of x

1 $3x = 12$
2 $x + 5 = 8$
3 $4x = 24$
4 $x + 5 = 6$
5 $4x = 10$
6 $2x = 15$
7 $6 + x = 9$
8 $3x = 21$
9 $x - 5 = 9$
10 $12 = 4x$
11 $\dfrac{x}{2} = 14$
12 $8 = \dfrac{x}{2}$
13 $x - 5 = 8$
14 $7x = 28$
15 $9 = 10 - x$
16 $6 - x = 2$
17 $3 + x = 7$
18 $6 = 10 - x$
19 $6 = \dfrac{x}{3}$
20 $\dfrac{x}{5} = 5$

B Find the value of x

1 $3x + 1 = 16$
2 $4 + 2x = 12$
3 $2x + 3 = 4$
4 $5 + 3x = 11$
5 $5x + 6 = 26$
6 $x - 9 = 15$
7 $2x + 5 = 8$
8 $7 + 3x = 22$
9 $5x - 3 = 17$
10 $2x - 5 = 11$
11 $6x - 4 = 20$
12 $7 + 2x = 10$
13 $3 - x = 2$
14 $5 - 2x = 1$
15 $27 - 2x = 15$
16 $2x - 3 = 8$
17 $2 + 3x = 5$
18 $9 - 2x = 6$
19 $4x + 1 = 17$
20 $5 + 3x = 20$

C Find the value of x

1 $2(x + 1) = 8$
2 $3(x - 2) = 9$
3 $5(x + 2) = 30$
4 $6(x - 4) = 12$
5 $4(x + 3) = 20$
6 $3(x - 1) = 21$
7 $5(x - 2) = 0$
8 $2(x + 3) = 7$
9 $4(x - 4) = 12$
10 $3(x + 5) = 18$
11 $2(3x - 4) = 22$
12 $5(3 + 3x) = 15$
13 $2(5x - 7) = 26$
14 $3(4x - 10) = 12$
15 $2(2x - 1) = 4$
16 $6(2 + x) = 30$
17 $4(x + 1) - 2 = 10$
18 $5 + 2(3x - 8) = 13$
19 $4(5x - 9) - 4 = 0$
20 $5(1 + 3x) - 5 = 30$

D 1 A shopkeeper is making himself a chart to show how much VAT he has charged. He uses a formula $\dfrac{3 \times P}{23}$ where P is the price in pounds which the customer has paid. Copy and complete this part of the chart:

Price paid by customer	£10	£20	£25	£30	£35	£40
VAT included in price paid	£1.30					

2 A manufacturer has split the cost of producing a certain product and displayed the ratios like this:

	raw materials : labour : other expenses		
ratio	9 parts	7 parts	4 parts
costs	£180 000	£x	£y

Calculate the cost £x for labour.
Calculate the total cost of the product.

EXAMPLE

$2(x + 3) = 2x + 6$
$5(2 - 4x) = 10 - 20x$

$$2(x + 3) + 5x = 2x + 6 + 5x$$
$$= 7x + 6$$

A Simplify

1 $3(x + 4)$
2 $5(2 + 3x)$
3 $4(2y - 5)$
4 $2(x + y)$
5 $6(2x + 1)$
6 $3(5 - 3y)$
7 $5(2k + 3)$
8 $3(h + 3k - 1)$
9 $6(6 - 2a)$
10 $5(4b - 2)$
11 $3(c + 2d)$
12 $2(a - 1 + 3c)$
13 $4(s + 3t)$
14 $10(n - 1)$
15 $5(x - 2y)$
16 $4(x + 3 + y)$
17 $2(3a - 3 + c)$
18 $3(4 + b)$
19 $2(3b - c + 2)$
20 $3(5x - 4)$

B Simplify

1 $2(x + 3) + 4x$
2 $3(y - 1) - 2$
3 $5(2x + y) + 2y$
4 $2x + 3(x - 5)$
5 $4a + 2(a + 3)$
6 $3(y + 2) - 6$
7 $4(3 + 2a) - 10$
8 $4x + 5(2 + x)$
9 $6 + 2(s - 3)$
10 $5x + 2(x - 1)$
11 $3x + 3(1 - y)$
12 $a + 3(b + 1)$
13 $2(x - 2) - x$
14 $5k + 3(2 - k)$
15 $4a + 3(a - 2b)$
16 $8 + 2(3d - 4)$
17 $x + 3 + 2(x - 1)$
18 $7 + h + 5(h + 1)$
19 $2(x - y) + 7y$
20 $3(4 - a) - 10 + 5a$

C Find the value of x in these sequences:

1 $2, 6, 10, x, 18, 22, 26$
2 $3, 6, 9, 12, x, 18, 21$
3 $15, x, 13, 12, 11, 10$
4 $4, 9, 14, x, 24, 29$
5 $15, 19, 23, x, 31, 35$

6 $1, 2, 9, 16, x, 36, 49$
7 $100, 90, 80, x, 60, 50$
8 $1, 2, 4, 8, 16, x, 64$
9 $64, 61, 58, 55, x, 49, 46$
10 $1, 8, 15, 22, x, 36, 43$

EXAMPLE

If $p = 3$ and $q = 7$

$2p = 2 \times 3 \quad 5q = 5 \times 7$
$\quad = 6 \qquad \qquad = 35$
$p^2 = 3 \times 3 \quad 4q + 1 = 4 \times 7 + 1$
$\quad = 9 \qquad \qquad \quad = 28 + 1$
$\qquad \qquad \qquad \qquad = 29$

If $k = 4$, $h = -2$, $m = 3$

$km = 4 \times 3 \quad 5h = 5 \times (-2)$
$\quad = 12 \qquad \qquad = -10$
$m + h = 3 + (-2)$
$\quad = 3 - 2$
$\quad = 1$

A Find the value of the following when
$a = 2, b = 5, c = \frac{1}{2}, d = 0, e = 4$

1 $2a$

2 $4b$

3 $6c$

4 $5a$

5 $3b$

6 $4d$

7 b^2

8 e^2

9 $2e$

10 $4c$

11 $3a + 1$

12 $2e - 3$

13 $d + e$

14 $e^2 + 3$

15 $4e + d$

16 $5 + a$

17 $4 + 3b$

18 $3 + 5a$

19 $7 + 2b$

20 $2c + b$

B Find the value of the following when
$x = 3, y = -4, s = -3, t = 8$

1 $6x$

2 $4t$

3 $2s$

4 $5y$

5 x^3

6 $3y$

7 xy

8 st

9 sx

10 tx

11 $7 + y$

12 $1 + x^2$

13 $t + s$

14 $3 + 2t$

15 $t + x$

16 $2x + 5$

17 $2x - 5$

18 $2s + t$

19 $t^2 - 4$

20 $5t - 4$

C 1

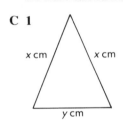

The perimeter of this triangle is $(2x + y)$ cm. When x is 5 and y is 7 what are the lengths of the sides? Use the formula to calculate the perimeter of this triangle.

2

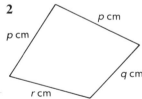

Write down a formula for the perimeter of this shape. When $p = 5$, $q = 6$ and $r = 7$, calculate its perimeter.

3 Three sisters are p years, q years and r years old. Next year they will be $(p + 1)$ years, $(q + 1)$ years and $(r + 1)$ years old. The formula for their average age next year is $\dfrac{p + q + r + 3}{3}$

If their ages now are 4, 7 and 13 years, use the formula to find their average age next year.

4 Mr Brown is a newsagent. He charges his customers 20p a week for delivering their papers. He uses the formula £$\dfrac{S + 6D + 20}{100}$ to work out the weekly bill for each customer. D is the cost in pence of the daily paper and S pence is the cost of the Sunday paper.

Fred Smith's daily paper costs 40p and his Sunday paper costs 50p. How much will Mr Brown charge him?

Mrs Davies has a daily paper costing 50p and Sunday papers costing 90p. Use the formula to find her bill.

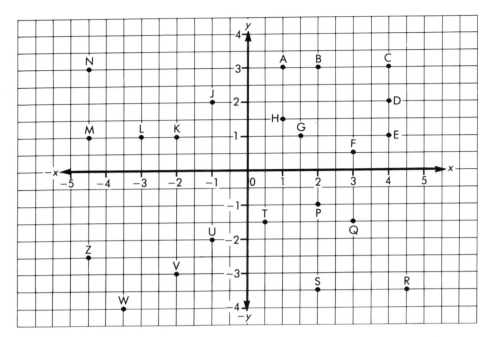

A The co-ordinates of the point A are (1, 3). Write down the co-ordinates of the other points, starting with B, then C, and so on.

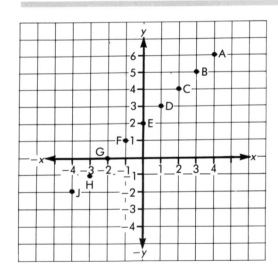

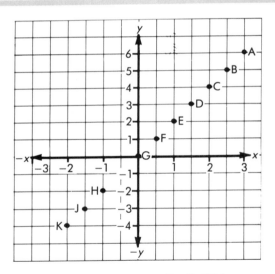

B The co-ordinates of A are (4, 6). Write down the co-ordinates of the other points, starting with B.

If the axes were long enough, when $x = 7$, what would y be?

What is the equation for finding y?

Check that all the co-ordinates obey the rule.

C The co-ordinates of A are (3, 6). Write down the co-ordinates of the other points, starting with B.

If the axes were long enough, when $x = 10$, what would y be?

What is the equation for finding y?

Check that all the co-ordinates obey the rule.

88

16 mixed practice papers

A
1. $27 - 14$
2. $27 \div 3$
3. $26p + 35p$
4. $17p - 9p$
5. $\frac{1}{2} = \frac{?}{4}$
6. $\frac{4}{10} = \frac{?}{5}$
7. $1.6 + 0.3$
8. $1.6 - 0.9$
9. Express $\frac{1}{2}$ as a percentage.
10. Express $\frac{1}{4}$ as a percentage.
11. Find the average of 6 and 8.
12. $5x + 4x$
13. $7x - 3x$
14. Find the perimeter of a rectangle 4 cm long by 3 cm wide.
15. Find the area of a rectangle 5 cm long and 4 cm wide.
16. Find the volume of a cube of edge 3 cm.
17. Write down an even factor of 70.
18. Write 15.30 hours using am or pm.
19. In triangle ABC, $\angle A = 30°$, $\angle B = 57°$. Calculate $\angle C$.
20. Which of these are multiples of 5: 51, 25, 45?

B
1. $29 - 15$
2. $32 \div 4$
3. $16p + 39p$
4. $15p - 9p$
5. $\frac{1}{3} = \frac{?}{6}$
6. $\frac{6}{8} = \frac{?}{4}$
7. $1.7 + 0.04$
8. $3.2 - 0.8$
9. Express $\frac{1}{5}$ as a percentage.
10. Find 25% of 28.
11. Find the average of 7 and 13.
12. $6x + 9x$
13. $9x - 2x$
14. Find the perimeter of a rectangle 6 cm long and 4 cm wide.
15. Find the area of a rectangle 9 cm long by 6 cm wide.
16. Find the volume of a cube of edge 5 cm.
17. Write down an even factor of 46.
18. Write 18.15 hours using am or pm.
19. In triangle ABC, $\angle A = 48°$, $\angle B = 60°$. Calculate $\angle C$.
20. Which of these are multiples of 6: 14, 18, 12?

C
1. $47 - 14$
2. $28 \div 4$
3. $17p + 19p$
4. $45p - 22p$
5. $\frac{1}{4} = \frac{?}{12}$
6. $\frac{8}{10} = \frac{?}{5}$
7. $2.01 + 0.04$
8. $4.6 - 1.2$
9. Express $\frac{3}{4}$ as a percentage.
10. Find 20% of 30.
11. Find the average of 9 and 13.
12. $7x + 6x$
13. $11x - 4x$
14. Calculate the perimeter of a rectangle of length 9 cm and breadth 6 cm.
15. Find the area of a rectangle of length 7 cm and breadth 6 cm.
16. Find the volume of a cube of edge 4 cm.
17. Write down an even factor of 74.
18. Write 11.45 hours using am or pm.
19. In triangle ABC, $\angle A = 67°$, $\angle B = 80°$. Calculate $\angle C$.
20. Which of these are multiples of 8: 16, 18, 24?

A

1 742 − 119

2 34 × 5

3 39 ÷ 3

4 £1.67 + £1.79

5 £1 − 60p

6 $\frac{3}{5} + \frac{4}{5}$ as a mixed number.

7 0.2 × 3

8 8.4 ÷ 2

9 Express $\frac{3}{8}$ as a percentage.

10 Find 30% of 60.

11 Find the average of 2, 3 and 4.

12 $7x - 8x$

13 Find the perimeter of a square of side 7 cm.

14 Find the area of a square of side 9 cm.

15 Find the volume of a cuboid of length 6 cm, breadth 2 cm and height 3 cm.

16 Divide one thousand by forty.

17 Write down a prime factor of 63.

18 Write 9.15 pm using the 24-hour clock.

19 In triangle PQR, $\angle P = 86°$, $\angle Q = 78°$. Which is the longest side?

20 Which of these are prime numbers: 11, 15, 17?

B

1 654 − 137

2 37 × 6

3 40 ÷ 5

4 £1.76 + £1.19

5 £1 − 70p

6 $\frac{5}{9} + \frac{5}{9}$ as a mixed number.

7 0.3 × 4

8 8.2 ÷ 2

9 Express $\frac{5}{8}$ as a percentage.

10 Find 30% of 80.

11 Find the average of 5, 6 and 7.

12 $5x - 9x$

13 Calculate the perimeter of a square of side 9 cm.

14 Find the area of a square of side 6 cm.

15 What is the volume of a cuboid of length 4 cm, breadth 3 cm and height 3 cm?

16 Divide seven thousand five hundred by sixty.

17 Write down a prime factor of 45.

18 Write 11.45 pm using the 24-hour clock.

19 In triangle PQR, $\angle P = \angle 48°$, $\angle Q = 68°$. Which is the longest side?

20 Which of these are prime numbers: 7, 23, 27?

C

1 786 − 129

2 32 × 8

3 42 ÷ 7

4 £1.85 + £2.76

5 £1 − 90p

6 $\frac{4}{5} + \frac{4}{5}$ as a mixed number.

7 0.5 × 3

8 4.62 ÷ 2

9 Express $\frac{7}{8}$ as a percentage.

10 Find 30% of 90.

11 Find the average of 6, 8 and 10.

12 $7x - 12x$

13 Find the perimeter of a square of side 5 cm.

14 Find the area of a square of side 7 cm.

15 What is the volume of a cuboid of length 8 cm, breadth 4 cm and height 2 cm?

16 Divide five thousand and forty by eighty.

17 Write down the largest prime factor of 57.

18 Write 9.30 pm using the 24-hour clock.

19 In triangle PQR, $\angle P = 63°$, $\angle Q = 65°$. Which is the shortest side?

20 Which of these are prime numbers: 5, 21, 23?

A

1. A man is paid £6600 a year. How much is that a month?
2. 999×17
3. $450 \div 25$
4. How many cm in a metre?
5. Express 2.716 correct to 2 decimal places.
6. Write down the square root of 144.
7. $(9)^2$
8. If $x = 3$, find $5x^2$.
9. If $ax = y$, express x in terms of a and y.
10. Find the volume of a cube of edge 9 cm.
11. How do you find the perimeter of a rectangle given the area and one side?
12. Find the marked angle:

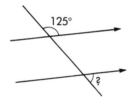

13. Find the total length of the edges of a 6 cm cube.
14. Find the total surface area of a 6 cm cube.
15. Calculate the volume of a right prism if the end area is 8 cm^2 and the length is 5 cm.
16. 125×8
17. Express £2.50 as a fraction of £12.50.
18. Divide 12 cm in the ratio 3:5.
19. What fraction is 7 of 28?
20. $4x - 3 = 25$, find x.

B

1. A man earns £5000 a year. How much, approximately, is this a month?
2. 999×23
3. $750 \div 25$
4. How many metres are there in a kilometre?
5. Express 3.7142 correct to 2 decimal places.
6. Write down the square root of 1.44.
7. $(0.9)^2$
8. If $x = 4$, find $3x^2$.
9. If $tx = k$, express x in terms of t and k.
10. Find the volume of a cuboid of length 7 cm, breadth 8 cm and height 6 cm.
11. Give the formula for finding the area of a triangle.
12. Find the missing angle:

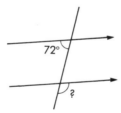

13. Find the total length of the edges of a 4 cm cube.
14. Find the total surface area of a 4 cm cube.
15. Calculate the volume of a right prism if the end area is 24 cm^2 and the length is 5 cm.
16. 125×16
17. Express £3.60 as a fraction of £36.
18. Divide 15 m in the ratio 1:4.
19. What fraction is 11 of 55?
20. $6x - 7 = 8$, find x.

C

1. A man earns £8000 a year. Approximately how much is this a month?
2. 999×45
3. $625 \div 25$
4. How many mm in a cm?
5. Express 4.56 correct to 2 significant figures.
6. Write down the square root of 1.21.
7. $(0.08)^2$
8. If $x = 5$, find $4x^2$.
9. If $mx = V$, express x in terms of m and V.
10. Find the volume of a cube of 12 cm.edge.
11. Give the formula for finding the volume of a right triangular prism.
12. Find the marked angle:

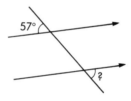

13. Find the total length of the edges of a 5 cm cube.
14. Find the total surface area of a 5 cm cube.
15. Calculate the volume of a right prism if the end area is 52 cm^2 and the length is 4 cm.
16. 125×24
17. Express £1.50 as a fraction of £7.50.
18. Divide 21 m in the ratio 1:2.
19. What fraction is 12 of 60?
20. $8x - 5 = 5$, find x.

A
1. 7.5×2000.
2. Write 34.58 correct to 1 decimal place.
3. Write 13.25 hours using am or pm.
4. Express $\frac{1}{10}$ as a %.
5. $22.5 \text{ cm} \times 200$ to nearest metre.
6. Express 1180 mm in cm.
7. Express $\frac{1}{10}$ as a decimal.
8. If $a = 8.5$, $b = 3$, find the value of $2a + b$.
9. Find 10% of 60.
10. Find the whole numbers which make $1 < x < 4$ a true statement.
11. Decrease 600 kg by 10%.
12. Write 3491 to the nearest ten.
13. Find the perimeter of a triangle with sides 8.5 cm, 9 cm, 8 cm.
14. When the temperature fell from 1°C to −2°C, how much did it fall?
15. Write the time 10 minutes after 11.50 am.
16. The sides of a rectangle are 8.5 cm and 3 cm. What is its area?
17. Find time it takes to travel 70 km at 20 km/h.
18. Write the next number 1, 4, 9, 16, . . .
19. Express 70% as a decimal.
20. Write a statement about 69.16 and 69.18.

B
1. 3.5×4000.
2. Write 63.27 correct to 1 decimal place.
3. Write 14.45 hours using am or pm.
4. Express $\frac{1}{20}$ as a %.
5. $10.5 \text{ cm} \times 400$ to nearest metre.
6. Express 780 mm in cm.
7. Express $\frac{1}{20}$ as a decimal.
8. If $a = 4.5$, $b = 5$, find the value of $2a + b$.
9. Find 30% of 120.
10. Find the whole numbers which make $3 < x < 6$ a true statement.
11. Decrease 1000 kg by 10%.
12. Write 6360 to the nearest ten.
13. Find the perimeter of a triangle with sides 4.5 cm, 5 cm, 4 cm.
14. When the temperature fell from 4°C to −4°C, how much did it fall?
15. Write the time 20 minutes after 11.50 am.
16. The sides of a rectangle are 4.5 cm and 5 cm. What is its area?
17. Find time it takes to travel 130 km at 20 km/h.
18. Write the next number 30, 60, 90, 120, . . .
19. Express 30% as a decimal.
20. Write a statement about 126.54 and 126.56.

C
1. $650 \text{ kg} \div 10$.
2. Write 46.07 correct to 1 decimal place.
3. What is the time $1\frac{1}{2}$ hours after 11.45 am?
4. Express $\frac{1}{4}$ as a %.
5. $45.5 \text{ g} \times 100$ to nearest kg.
6. Express 1080 cl in litres.
7. Express $\frac{3}{5}$ as a decimal.
8. If $a = 7.5$, $b = 2$, find the value of $10a - b$.
9. Find 20% of 30 tons.
10. Solve $2 + x = 5$.
11. Increase 400 by 10%.
12. Write 4640 to the nearest hundred.
13. Find the perimeter of a rectangle with sides 7.5 cm, 9 cm.
14. Share £1.60 in the ratio 1:3.
15. Write the time 5 minutes after 1.10 pm.
16. The sides of a rectangle are 7.5 cm and 2 cm. What is its area?
17. How long does it take to travel 4 km at 5 km/h?
18. Write the next number 1, 2, 8, 27, . . .
19. Express 60% as a decimal.
20. Two angles of a triangle are 10° and 60°. Find the third angle.

D
1. $320 \text{ kg} \div 20$.
2. Write 707.09 correct to 1 decimal place.
3. What is the time $1\frac{1}{2}$ hours after 10.25 am?
4. Express $\frac{1}{8}$ as a %.
5. $22.4 \text{ g} \times 200$ to nearest kg.
6. Express 750 cl in litres.
7. Express $\frac{3}{10}$ as a decimal.
8. If $a = 4.2$, $b = 3$, find the value of $10a - b$.
9. Find 30% of 60 tons.
10. Solve $3 + x = 7$.
11. Increase 600 by 10%.
12. Write 70742 to the nearest hundred.
13. Find the perimeter of a rectangle with sides 4.2 cm, 5.7 cm.
14. Share 1.5 m in the ratio 2:3.
15. Write the time 10 minutes after 1.10 pm.
16. The sides of a rectangle are 4.2 cm and 3 cm. What is its area?
17. How long does it take to travel 7 km at 5 km/h?
18. Write the next number 7, 21, 28, 35, 42, . . .
19. Express 27% as a decimal.
20. Two angles of a triangle are 20° and 60°. Find the third angle.